A Day at a Time

A Day at a Time

BEPPIE HARRISON

Bookcraft
Salt Lake City, Utah

Library of Congress Catalog Card Number: 93-74924
ISBN 0-88494-918-4

First Printing, 1994

Printed in the United States of America

To my sisters,
Martha and Barbara,
for all the past, present, and future that we share

Contents

1

On Living a Day at a Time

Getting discouraged is the kind of thing that can creep up on you.

It creeps up on me, particularly on the days when I have done two or three stupid things in a row, or haven't done a bunch of things I know I ought to have done, or feel guilty because my spiritual life seems to have lapsed into a plodding routine, or am just feeling what my mother-in-law calls "off color." On those days often the weather is unhelpful, as well: it seems much easier to get discouraged when it's overcast and drizzling outside (which means wet feet and muddy footprints down the back hall) or towards the end of winter when the snow is grimy and crusty with hard, icy bumps on the edges of everything and I'm so dreadfully tired of coats and gloves and tugging on boots. Because lying down on the living room couch and feeling sorry for myself is not really a practical possibility, I try to take my willpower by the nape of the neck and keep moving regardless, but on those discouraging days I don't seem to see the things I accomplish. I see the things I don't get to; I see the rough edges of the things I didn't finish properly—including the scriptures I rushed over and the prayers that fell into formula; I see, with crystal clarity, every scintilla of noncooperation from anybody around me and respond defensively, bristling.

Through it all, there is one thing that seems manifestly obvious on those frustrating, discouraging days. Somehow it is all my fault. If I were better organized, I would get everything done. If I were more thorough, I would get my jobs wholly completed instead of almost done, with loose ends tucked hastily under. If I were a better person (whatever that might mean), I would be capable of genuine spirituality, I could inspire other people to spontaneous helpfulness, my children would pick up their own belongings and do all their homework, and my husband and I would understand each other all the time and never get testy.

Now, on good days I know there are a few holes in that argument, but on discouraging days it all seems to flow quite sensibly. "If I were just good enough," I tell myself gloomily. "If I were as good as . . . ," and I run forlornly through my list of other people who apparently excel at whatever it is that I am most discouraged about. "She has no problem getting organized"—or getting things done, or being spiritual enough, or whatever it is I am feeling incapable of that particular wet Wednesday. And there I am, arriving at the only possible conclusion. I am just plain not good enough.

For a long time I believed I was the only person who thought this way, even a day at a time. And then I started listening to people. I started listening to the good sisters in my ward. I started listening to the other moms gossiping as we waited to pick up our kids from one activity or another. I started paying more attention to the avalanche of magazine and newspaper articles about women, all of them offering suggestions on how each of us individually can become more competent at this or that and consequently discover richer, more satisfying lives and feel better about ourselves. It began to dawn on me that a lot of women are familiar with the feeling that they are falling short here or there along the line, that somehow they just aren't measuring up.

When I started asking my friends—tentatively at first, because they were the very ones who looked to be in such comfortable command of their lives—I discovered that they, too, had days when they wondered, days when they measured the gap between where they are and where they want to be and found it infinitely wide. They, too, had days when they felt they weren't good enough. And if none of them are good enough—these ordinary, busy women who run families and hold down jobs and organize fund-raisers for good causes and bake bread and quilt quilts and keep the Church auxiliaries and the volunteer arm of our communities ticking over—then who is? And what is "good enough" anyway?

It occurs to me that it's as if there's a race out there. We can see the pack out ahead of us—even if we can't identify precisely who's in it—but we don't seem to be able to catch up with it. On good days, when the sun shines and things fall into place comfortably, we jog along contentedly in spite of being behind. On especially good days, we may even catch the scent of the flowers and the fresh coolness of the breeze in our hair. On days like that, who's in the pack ahead—or even that there is a pack—doesn't seem so important. Things get done (James's hair cut, check; kitchen floor scrubbed, check; job project turned in, check; Sunday's lesson prepared—and this is only Tuesday—check, oh, glorious check), and tomorrow's list can be coped with tomorrow.

It's on the discouraging days that I lose that sense of serenity, and focus forlornly on the gap between my achievements and my intentions. The pack seems to be moving farther and farther ahead, and when I try to sprint out to catch up, I stumble over my own exasperating shortcomings. I should be kinder. I should be more patient. I should be more generous with my time and my commitments. I should be a more faithful daughter of my Father in Heaven. I should just plain be a better person. Am I alone in feeling this way?

It's not that I don't know the eternal truths, somewhere down in the marrow of my bones. In my heart of hearts I know, as I know the arching sky over my head is real, that I am a daughter of God and that as a daughter of God I have unlimited potential. On good days, that is gloriously good enough. I tuck my potential back under my arm more securely and have another try at catching up to where I ought to be.

So what is it about the bad days, the down days, the discouraging days? Why can't I be mindful of my potential on the bad days? What is it about them that makes me feel so bleak?

Clearly, this isn't the way we are meant to feel. We have been told that "men are, that they might have joy" (2 Nephi 2:25)— and "men" here obviously means mortal beings in general, not just the male ones. The feeling of forlorn futility that comes on discouraging days is a good long distance from joy, that's for certain.

But if feeling discouraged isn't the intended destination, maybe it is a more or less inevitable way station. We have a lot of jobs during our time here on earth, and since we are mortal it is unlikely we will execute them all flawlessly all the time. We are daughters first, then sisters, wives, mothers,—and aunts, cousins, and nieces, depending on how our particular family patchwork is laid out. So, we have all the complications of human relationships to grapple with.

We are now, and traditionally have been, housekeepers, homemakers, and tenders of the hearth—unless the hearth is outside and called a barbecue, in which case most of us just supply raw materials and let our husbands play. Lately some women do a lot of other things as well. A few of us are captains of industry. Some of us are professionals in our own right; a lot more of us are distributed up and down the skilled and semi-skilled ladder; and some of us have few marketable skills but still need to bring a paycheck home, just as the men around us have always needed to do. But in an important sense, what precise circumstances make up the framework of our individual lives is simply a detail. What we are here to do most fundamentally, no matter where we fit in the social pattern, is to learn to choose. We have been sent to earth to make our own choices based on what we learn here, and inevitably, as part of the learning process, we sometimes make the wrong ones.

It is almost impossible to overemphasize how important those choices are. If we make enough wrong choices—and stick to them stubbornly enough—we can destroy ourselves. In a way, we're like babies fascinated by a fire. From time to time, and in the virtually infinite variety of ways dictated by our own individuality, each of us will stick our fingers into the flames and get scorched. Getting scorched is *not* a joyful experience. The baby sucks her burnt fingers and cries. In the bleak sterility of the discouraging days, is there maybe some vague spiritual equivalent to sucking scorched fingers?

Nor are our mistakes the only difficulties we have to deal with. Everybody has trials. Everybody always did. Everybody has to live a day at a time. My great-grandmother walked a lot of the way across the plains. Before she did that, she had to go through the anxiety of hovering on the edges while her parents, sustained only by their new faith in what the early missionaries had taught them, sold what they could and packed up everything else that was familiar and launched into the unknown. For herself, she was able to bring only her doll; the doll sits on my chest of drawers now, staring at me with her china eyes and smiling her china smile that comforted my great-grandmother. Once Great-Grandmother got to Utah, her life was still hard in many ways. When she died, her hands showed a lifetime of labor.

Before her, her grandmother lived in a changing England that was turning from rural stability to the promises and perils of industrialization. My ancestors were undoubtedly much like their neighbors (in school we learn about the kings and queens of England, but then, as now, most people were common, ordinary people leading common, anonymous lives). They lived in a smoky, sooty world where days were long and dangerous. Men faced the hazards of unregulated toil on the farm or with the new factory machines; a lot of women did, too. No matter where she worked, a woman faced the peril of childbirth. Survival could not be taken for granted. Even if she did survive, some of her children would not. Disease was a familiar companion, and people died young.

And before her—what of her grandmother? It's hard to imagine. Certainly she lived in a more stable world, but by her birth she would have been locked into her place in it, among the poor or among the well-to-do. I doubt she had many choices about where to live or whom to marry. Disease would have stalked her also and whomever she loved. She would have had few physical comforts: no furniture beyond maybe a stool, a chest, and a bed, if they were particularly prosperous; plain clothing, spun at home. I hope she was warm against the damp chill of the English winter.

Whatever their circumstances, those women, my ancestors, came to mortality—as I have come—and learned what was available to them to learn. Compared to the physical difficulties they endured, I live in voluptuous luxury. My house is heated in

the winter and cooled in the summer. It is full of soft, uphol-
stered furniture and carpets to comfort bare feet. (They may be
a little shabby compared to some of my neighbors' furnishings,
but they're still a far cry from a wooden stool or an earthen
floor.) My wardrobe may not be jewel bedecked, but I have
more clothes than most court ladies of their time would have
dreamed of, and without doubt my clothes are easier to move
around in.

Machinery does a lot of the heavy work my foremothers
did. I don't have to tend a fire; I turn on the stove or adjust the
thermostat. There is water whenever I want it, one tap for hot
and another for cold. My food is kept chilled and available out
of season in my refrigerator, and the only ice involved is the
amount I choose to make. Downstairs in the basement, two
white cubes wash and dry the family's clothes. If I want to create a romantic atmosphere I may light a candle, but I flick a
switch for light to find where I put the candles and to hunt for
the matches.

So what are my trials? How dare I sit in what has to be,
comparatively speaking, a palace and, on the discouraging days,
suck on my scorched fingers and feel sorry for myself? I would
venture to suggest that maybe the trials we face—as Latter-day
Saint women struggling through the tail end of the twentieth
century—are of a different kind altogether. Our physical circumstances may be easier than were those of our forebears, but
they threw the book at us when it came to making choices.
Want a little free agency? Have a bunch.

Where do you want to live? Whom do you want to marry?
To a degree unparalleled in the experience of our ancestors, it's
up to us. Do you want opportunities for using your mind, for
education? Down the centuries, education has been the privi-
lege of the few, seldom including any women. Now almost
everybody, male and female, has schooling available. Even the
kids today who resist every assignment know more than their
wisest forefathers knew.

What do we want to do with our labor? Traditionally, women
have had few choices. Even the most powerful were locked into
expectations. Elizabeth the Great raged at her ministers who
were seeking to control her early in her career. They expected
her to marry and become a wife—a royal one, naturally, but

obedient to a husband. Elizabeth prevailed, partly through circumstance and partly through iron determination, and ruled as a woman, but at the price of dying childless and unmarried. For her time, she was an anomaly.

Now we can usually freely choose. Although most women still marry and have children, the choice to work outside the home is available. In fact, for many women, the choice to stay at home is ruled out by unyielding economic reality. Women are an accepted part of the work force. For some, this opens wonderful new horizons. The capable, ambitious woman who has not married finds herself able to compete with men in a workplace more hospitable to her than ever before. Unfortunately, the capable, ambitious woman who has family responsibilities but who may have to work discovers she is an involuntary pioneer in the great experiment of merging wholly divergent expectations and necessities.

Oh, yes indeed, we have choices. Maybe one of *our* trials is that we have to make the choices in a society in which none of the choices are universally accepted as the right choice for a woman to make. It's not hard to get discouraged sometimes when people are noisily pointing out that what you're doing is misguided—and whatever you do, in our times, there are bound to be people who think it's misguided.

If you choose to find fulfillment in being a wife and a mother at home, there are people to suggest that you are disregarding your individual potential and probably lacking the gumption to do anything else. If you choose to live independently, you will hear the murmurs that you are ignoring what should be your most important priorities. If you marry, your identity is swallowed up by that of your husband (they say); if you don't, you have somehow come up short—the wallflower, the unchosen. What's most irritating is that the unspoken assumption seems to be that all women have all the choices freely available at all times. We *do* have unparalleled choices over the course of our lifetimes, but most of us have to make our own particular choices at any one time on the basis of what presents itself at the right moment. Maybe Prince Charming does arrive on cue—or at least a reasonable facsimile. Maybe he doesn't. Maybe a job comes along instead, a rather ordinary one that, like a Chinese box, opens up in unexpected ways and, with luck, turns into a challenge and a delight. Maybe Prince Charming presented himself, but not the "happily ever after," and suddenly there you are with the children, looking for a job.

We have other significant choices to make. We live blessed by the fulness of the gospel, and Jesus told his original disciples—and repeated to Joseph Smith in later revelation—"For unto whomsoever much is given, of him shall be much required" (Luke 12:48; see also D&C 82:3). Generations of good women were given little and expected to be faithful only to that little. We have been given vastly more, and our responsibilities are correspondingly greater. We know our place in the eternal pattern: we know that the counsel of the prophets, ancient and modern, forms the foundation of the expectations that we shape our choices to meet.

As eternal beings who know we are eternal, we are not limited by this world, and even less so by the particular society in which we are born and spend our days. Reaching over and beyond the details of daily existence—the details of being housewives or accountants, married or single, childless or surrounded by insistent small hands—we have a wholly singular relationship with our Father in Heaven, and within that relationship we have the commandment that is infinitely more ambitious even than being good enough to climb past this step of mortality. We have been commanded to be perfect.

Being simply good enough to get by seems unlikely enough on the discouraging days. Being perfect? Inevitably, the mind boggles at this thought. When we face the image of perfection, there is not one of us that is good enough, not even on the absolutely best-of-a-lifetime day.

After all, what is *good,* anyhow? It seems odd, but fitting, to learn that centuries ago the Sanskrit word that came to be the foundation of the English word *good* meant "to hold fast." Perhaps that's part of what *good* still means to us: to hold fast to our obligations, to our responsibilities, to the commandments.

Good, as we use it normally, implies a lot of things. It certainly includes the idea of competence. Often, on those discouraging days when I don't feel good enough, what I'm mourning is my lack of competence. Being good at things— being competent—makes life move more efficiently. It is easier to repair a fence or to put up curtains if you know how to do it and have developed the basic skills. Obviously everybody has to learn certain skills sometime, and no doubt we all hope to continue to gain competence our whole lives long, but taking the trouble to learn how to do well what we have to do is the essential first step. Much of what we do on a day-to-day basis—and certainly much of what we spend our time teaching our children—is centered around the skills that make a smoother, less accident-prone existence. The hitch is, of course, that it is much more fun to do the things we want to do, so there are those of us who are demonstrably more competent at gardening or knitting or woodworking or whatever than at darning socks or keeping rooms tidy or washing the woodwork.

We work at the skills of getting along with our fellow beings. We teach (and reteach and reteach) the principles of politeness to our impatient children in the hopes that observing the forms of consideration for others will encourage the reality. We try to learn to govern our own tongues, to keep still when the words on the tip of our tongues are cross or unkind. We struggle at the job of developing unselfishness, trying to think at least as much of others as we do of ourselves. (Of course, it's relatively easy to do that with the people we love already, but we have been admonished to widen our generosity beyond that tight circle.)

But there we seem to be shading over into another meaning of *good:* being good in the sense of being virtuous, of moral excellence rather than mortal competence. Virtue implies more than being good *at* something; it's just plain *being* good.

Here, in our relentlessly secular world, we're pretty much on our own. The makers of opinion here at the end of the twentieth century don't seem to think much about virtue, somehow. Reading the newspapers or listening to the burbling talk shows, you get the impression that nobody seems to take the notion of virtuous living as a particularly relevant concept. We are unsurprised to discover that any hero has spots; in fact, if we don't happen to notice the spots ourselves, there is a whole industry devoted to pointing them out. The general climate of opinion would seem to be that vaguely meaning well is about as much as ordinary people should be expected to do.

Not that only members of the Church are concerned with the challenges of doing good as well as being good. The finest minds the world has known have grappled with that problem down through the centuries, and in less cynical times than our own they have been admired for doing so. There are good people all around us working quietly away at the daily business of being virtuous. They might not have the light we would share with them, but they are using the light they do have. Unfortunately, the most vocal people seem to be the ones who figure that just plain getting along as long as you don't get in other people's way is as close to virtue as you need to be; and it's their point of view that we seem to see reflected in our movies and television programs and other media, which shape our opinions more than we like to recognize.

As obedient daughters of our Heavenly Father, blessed with the restored gospel, that worldly view can't be our point of view. We may not always get it right, but we have to aim at more than simply getting by. We have been commanded to aim for perfection.

We were all unique individuals before we came here, and our singularity is demonstrated in our widely varying reactions to the commandment to be perfect. Some of us find it easier to accept than others. All of us, I suspect, find it easier to work on at some times than at other times. Some of us work steadily and industriously, and some of us go in fits and starts. Some of us get more discouraged than others; some of us hit more obvious bumps in the road.

But all of us have the same task set: we must practice perfection while we are coping with the ordinary dailiness of life. Maybe it would be easier to practice perfection in the peace and silence of a convent, closed away from the complications and tumult of family life; maybe it would be easier still in the isolation of the empty desert, where so many philosophers in the first centuries after Christ searched for truth. That might be, but that's not what is asked of us. We have to practice perfection in the middle of everything else. We have to "hold fast" surrounded by dishes that need doing, babies that need changing, friends and associates who can be irritable, husbands who have problems of their own, and bodies that force limitations upon us.

Our job is to try to be good enough, to stretch toward perfection. We know we won't reach it; we knew that before we ever came here. Our Father's plan—the plan we accepted in the premortal life—was predicated on the knowledge that we would fall short. The safety net is in place. All we have to do is step out along the tightrope of obedience and take it a day at a time. No matter how many times we miss our step and fall, we can keep the resolution and the courage to climb back up again. God has promised he will stay with us, as long as we hold the faith that he is there and as long as we keep trying—really trying—to be what he has asked us to be. Even though we may not be able to see him, we can still hear his voice in the silence of our own thoughts. As long as we believe, he will sustain us.

Satan is there too, of course, dancing along just ahead of us on the tightrope, whispering to us all the time. He reminds us how high the rope is, how clumsy we are, how alone we feel, how many times we've slipped and fallen already; and when, having tumbled yet again, we lie limp and discouraged in the net, Satan is triumphant. "You're not good enough," he croons. "You know it. Everybody knows it. You're not going to measure up"—and on and on until we defeat him by wearily clambering up to our feet and starting to climb, stubbornly, back up to the rope.

The falls are inevitable, but they still hurt. Sometimes the hurt is the vague dissatisfaction of the discouraging days; sometimes the hurt is piercing anguish. Whichever way it is, we have to dig down and find the faith that the good days will come again and that however solitary we may feel at the moment, we are never truly alone. Our Savior is always there. Bone deep, we know that.

So how do we translate that into the practice of our everyday lives? How do we comfort ourselves with his presence when we are dashing around trying to tidy things up and get off to work, or scrubbing at the baby oatmeal that has hardened like glue on the highchair? How do we lift ourselves out of the undefined gloom of the wet Wednesdays as we stare morosely out of the window at the unencouraging gray sky? How do we reclaim some of that joy that we know ought to be there?

Well, I don't know that I know, myself. I don't expect that there is a magic formula, a single method that would always work. I'm sure my great-grandmother and my triple great-grandmother would have loved a magic formula to whisk them past their trials, but I doubt that they discovered one. Maybe what we need to do instead is to finger through the materials of our ordinary lives, to determine what is usable and worth keeping and what we can profitably discard. Maybe we can take out and look at what's good about the good days and also examine the kinds of things that tip us into the discouraging ones. Maybe we can find our own answers, and our own successes, to lighten the burden of the bleak days. Maybe we can use the light of the good days, when the flowers smell fresh and the breeze ruffles our hair, and spread it out to brighten the dark ones.

Maybe we can begin where we are, on a wet Wednesday, and work it out together, a day at a time.

2

On What's Expected

There's no doubt that on those discouraging days, I feel I am falling short. But falling short of what?

Well, for one thing—if I'm going to be perfectly honest, and what is the point of talking about it if I'm not?—I fall short of the examples of good people around me. There are a lot of good women in the world. I know women who are real scripturalists—women who dive into their studies with zest and enthusiasm. I can think of one in particular who lights up when she talks about the gospel. I didn't know her particularly well until I was assigned to be one of her visiting teachers; then we had the chance to talk, and our monthly visit kept stretching out longer and longer as we compared notes on what we had been reading and thinking about. Later my route was changed, but I still look for chances for us to spend time together—for me to warm my heart at the cozy fire of her love for spiritual learning.

I know another sister who is a practical, down-to-earth incarnation of compassionate service. At one time she was the bishop's wife, but when he was released she carried on, in a way, still shepherding the overlooked and forlorn ones. She is wonderfully matter-of-fact, seldom fusses, and delivers funny stories with her casseroles. She gathers up the solitary people for Sunday dinner at her house. I don't know how she always knows who needs a helping hand; I suppose it's basically that she pays attention. Sometimes, watching her bustle comfortably from one person to another down a crowded hall on Sunday, I wonder if she started out being so sensitive to other people's needs, or if that is the sort of thing that you learn, like playing the piano, through constant daily practice?

Then there is my friend who lives up the street. We don't share the gospel, but we share a lot of other things. We go to soccer games to watch our daughters play and to chat absent-mindedly while the play ranges up and down the field; we volunteer together at PTA activities at school and grumble companionably about the amount of busywork that seems inevitably involved. Years and years ago we were Brownie Scout leaders together, and we find particular fascination now in watching how our little second-graders have bloomed into high school seniors—some buxom, some thin as reeds.

Over all these years, I have watched her cope uncomplainingly with crippling arthritis. She has had a hip and a knee replaced; her hands are twisted and distorted. She walks much more slowly now. When we cross the soccer field to the sidelines this season, we amble at her pace. She grumbles about PTA irrationality, but she never grumbles about her arthritis. We laugh a lot together, and occasionally when we're over in her kitchen she hands me a jar to open—without comment—or reaches for my arm to help her balance up or down a step. She is absolutely matter-of-fact about either; I have never seen in her a flicker of self-pity. She is my model of patience and steadfast endurance; she puts up with what she must put up with and goes from there.

To truly love the scriptures, to put compassion into practice as naturally as breathing, to endure difficulties without complaining—those are only three of the virtues of good women who seem to be all around me. And there are all the others: I can point to the perfectly organized sister over there; to the effortlessly creative friend on the other side; to the gentle woman who seems to exist in a permanent atmosphere of unconditional love and acceptance of even the most difficult members of the ward. On the wet Wednesdays, instead of being inspired by their examples, I'm overwhelmed.

I want to be good in the ways they are good. But how do I go about it? When I was a child, I assumed that becoming good was something that came about automatically when you grew up. After all, my mother was good; so were the adults I associated with—or at least I was not encouraged to seek evidence that they were not. But here I am, by any measure thoroughly grown up, and I'm still waiting for goodness to creep over me of its own accord.

It's not that I don't know what I should be. *That* I know well.

I should be virtuous. My first impulse, not the afterthought, should be the generous one. I should want to serve others, even the unloving and unlovable ones. (As far as that goes, I shouldn't see people as unlovable—Christ didn't.) I should have skin color mean as little to me as eye color does, and I should stretch out my hand in respect to those whose lives are harder because of all of us who see them first as different and only second as our brethren. I should carry out my responsibilities in the ward and in the community without feeling hard done by on account of the number of meetings. I should be less enamored of my own way of going about things. I should be able to consistently carry out such a simple assignment as spending all day Sunday in appropriate activities with an appropriate attitude.

I should be joyfully obedient. I should keep the commandments instinctively, instead of being hassled by my own rebelliousness. I should not be inclined to expect that the Lord will bless me in the ways that seem most sensible to me. I should not turn my prayers into what can only be considered nagging, simply because in my tunnel vision I can see only one reasonable and logical solution to whatever my current difficulty might be. I should naturally and trustfully place the course of my life in the Lord's hands when everything is going smoothly, instead of turning to prayer most fervently when trouble is piling on trouble and I need help to know in what direction to go next.

I know I should do all those things and many others as well—how about consistently controlling my temper around the children, as a start?—and I've known it all my adult life. And how far have I gotten? On the discouraging days, it feels as if my progress is infinitesimal. Imperfection still flourishes in all aspects of my life, just like the weeds in my garden and the dirty finger marks on the woodwork. There is no dodging the plain conclusion: I'm just plain not good enough, yet.

Logically I know that part of the problem is the fact that, like most women, I live in a cat's cradle of expectations. There are not only the expectations that I am reminded of in Relief Society lessons but also all the other expectations that I pick up from the world. The world doesn't present those expectations as *lessons*, precisely; it's more a business of demonstrating, over and over, in the magazines and the newspapers, on television and the movie screen, what the world considers to be success.

For one thing, I'm supposed to be thin. For another, I'm supposed to be rich enough to buy all the things that are trotted out as desirable, hour after hour. My house is supposed to be in perfect order (can you think of any television program besides *Roseanne* that ever shows an untidy room?). I am supposed to cook with panache and in accordance with whatever the current nutritional wisdom might be. My problems are all readily resolvable—as long as I have the fashionable ones. There are experts upon experts (and they are multiplying faster than Australian rabbits) who each know exactly how I can deal with my problems. Everybody, in fact, seems to know exactly what I should be doing and figures all I need is some instruction and I'll snap into line and get my life running properly. Beauty, home management, career development, overseeing and guiding the psychological and physical development of my children, conduct of my marriage—everyone knows how it's done, and everyone is hustling to tell.

Sometimes I want to ask, loudly and impolitely, just when do I do it all? When and how am I supposed to fit it all in? Sometimes I am reminded of the delivery room, with everyone enthusiastically exhorting me to "push, push—push hard" (all of them, of course, fully dressed and in control of themselves, while I'm the one who's hot, disheveled, and who has this baby that has to get out). On the wet Wednesdays I want to shout back at the radio or the television, at the poised expert confidently explaining life to me, "I'm *trying!*" The trouble is that everyone is sure that if I just follow his or her directions I can accomplish everything—which means, of course, if I don't happen to be accomplishing everything right then I am clearly not measuring up. The really funny part is that on the wet Wednesdays, I buy it. I buy it hook, line, and sinker. ("Push, push hard.")

I expect, from time to time, we all buy it. Wives and mothers who are holding down outside jobs are assured by all the magazine articles and the talking heads on the multiplying talk shows that it is perfectly possible to keep a job going and still do all the important things at home. Nobody, naturally, suggests what tasks, other than perhaps dusting, may be considered unimportant at home. For women trying to keep on top of what amounts to two full-time jobs, dusting is seldom the major issue. Few of them are up until midnight checking the shine on the dining room table. What they *are* working away at feverishly as the night steadily gets shorter is getting the last load into the dryer or cooking some meals ahead to put in the freezer. Getting it done at all is a major accomplishment, but the experts too often convey the impression that that's the minimum bottom line. Surely you can manage centerpieces on the table and a dinner party on the weekend!

Women at home who manage a family on a single income in an economy geared to double-income families are made to feel that they should have plenty of time available for extras, in spite of the inescapable reality that doing practically anything cheaply involves spending a lot more time doing it, whether it's menu planning or grocery shopping or clothing the family or figuring out affordable recreation. Nor is life made more restful by the presence of babies and small children (and it's the presence of those babies and small children, generally, that governs their mother's decision to stay home in the first place), who too often sleep peacefully when their mother can't and wake shrieking during the few hours she has to spend in her own bed. But if you're home all day, the line goes, certainly you have plenty of time to catch a nap during the afternoon—and do the ironing, keep the house straight, read to the children, bake your own bread, fit in some volunteer work, polish the kitchen floor, and so on.

Of course, not all the expectations come from the world.

When we go to church on Sunday we have to deal with each
other, and each sister brings her own focus—and her own particular expectations—to our meetings. For one sister, genealogy
has central importance; for another, it's missionary work. Admiring their progress, we check guiltily on our own. How are
we doing? Are our charts in order, and have we identified families to introduce to the missionaries? Then there's temple atten-
dance, scripture study, food storage, homemaking skills, compassionate service, magnifying your callings, and devoting attention to and supervising your children's personal spiritual
progress—the list goes on and on. It's fatally easy to get the
feeling, when you're feeling a little daunted anyway, that not
only this world but the next as well are set up for people who
do everything a whole lot better than you are managing to do.

Maybe what we need to do is go home, go down on our
knees, and ask for a little common sense. We can't be everything to everybody, not all at once. Not only can't we do everything everybody expects us to do, we can't even do everything
we expect ourselves to accomplish. The expectations are coming from too many directions and from sources that have wildly
different agendas from our own. There is no way, for one thing,
that I can be both thin, elegant, trendy, and a cozy Mother
Earth with a lap. And after all, do I really want to be either one,
undiluted?

Eternity, we're told, goes on forever. One of the facts of
mortality is that it has limits. So we are forced to make choices,
and choices bring consequences. When we teach this principle
to our children, we simplify it into blacks and whites, but we
live in a world of grays. Our choices are often ambiguous ones,
bringing both the consequences we wanted and the ones we
wish didn't come along with the deal. We don't always take that
into consideration when we listen to the voices around us,
clamoring with their demands for us to get on with what they
say we should be doing.

You can't concentrate primarily on your own self-development
and simultaneously be a warm, nurturing hub of the family. In
the real world, neither priority automatically comes first. You
have to take turns. You can't devote the hours to exercise and
makeup and fashion that the movie and television stars do (no
wonder they look so good!) and keep up with a home and

family and maybe a job and still sleep at night—unless, like them, you maintain a paid domestic staff. On your own, you run out of hours. You can't even do everything you're taught to do in Relief Society, all at once. After you get past the basic core requirements—and they're pretty obvious—the rest works out to be something like "different strokes for different folks."

What happens is that inevitably we all make choices. What probably contributes to the wet Wednesday feeling is the sense that we're trying to do too much at once instead of taking command of what those choices are. When you're dashing at full speed from one obligation to the next, it's hard to evaluate whether the things you're doing are the things you wanted most to do or they're just simply what cropped up most obtrusively. You rushed off when teenage Abigail was trying to talk to you, because you had to get the book to the library before it closed today—or did you? If you'd taken a minute to consider, you would have realized that it would be only a ten-cent fine if you held on to the book until tomorrow and that it's been days since Abigail sought you out. But there you are, speeding down to the library as if the fate of civilization depended on the punctual return of that particular book, and Abigail has gone out, probably to talk to somebody else.

Those are the days when we most need to grasp back the sense of control. We need to step off the merry-go-round long enough to decide what's most important and what isn't. What we need to grasp hold of is our own particular method of clearing out the underbrush, of reminding ourselves of our own singular strengths and how they can be used to help us cope with our inadequacies.

We all have our strengths—even on the discouraging days when life is tossing us around. Some of us have been given the gift of patience and can stubbornly, triumphantly endure the difficulties we encounter. Some of us have been blessed with sharply insightful minds and can usually figure out how to manage things when we take the time to consider the matter. Some of us may be short on patience and given to muddy thinking under stress but be endowed with a sense of humor that enables us to bounce along like corks on river rapids. After all, once you've seen the funny side of a situation it's hard to be quite so convinced that everything is falling apart. These may not be the noblest virtues to have, and there's no doubt that sometimes the virtues that rescue us from gloom are distinctly odd, but then real life is sometimes very peculiar, too.

What rescues me may not necessarily work for you, and vice versa. We're not clones. If we were, we could each be given the never-fail recipe—one size fits all—that would solve every problem. Instead we're distinct individuals, and we have to work our solutions out for ourselves. We can certainly learn from each other. Indeed, one of the greatest practical strengths of the Church for us here in this mortal testing time is that it organizes and expands opportunities for us to learn from each other ways of coping with our individual challenges. But the only lessons that are really going to help us are the lessons that we— as unique spirits, daughters of our Heavenly Father—can use in our own lives, and the plain truth is that we may have to glean carefully from a lot of lessons to identify what we need most to use in our own lives right now.

I can learn from my sisters' accomplishments, but in my experience, I can't borrow those accomplishments the same way I would borrow a paper pattern to cut out a nightgown. What I learn has to be adapted, not duplicated. I've learned a great deal from one easygoing sister about how to cope with balky adolescents, and yet what my borrowed wisdom has produced is not a mirror image of the relationship she has with her children. Her example had to be tailored and modified to fit what was happening at my house with my children.

Sometimes, I suspect, the problem is that I expect myself to start out from the place that the people I admire have reached. Remember my scripturalist friend? Instead of spending a wet Wednesday blaming myself for not having acquired her knowledge and wisdom, perhaps it would be more useful to plan something less complicated for dinner and then sit down to use the time I've saved to do a bit of reading, and thinking, myself. Or, if what is haunting my mind is my inadequacy compared to the outpouring of service that my friend, the former bishop's wife, so freely dispenses, then maybe I should resolve to render some service to somebody (besides my family, who for the sake of the exercise won't count) every week, write down what I intend to do so I won't forget, and then do it. Or, if what I'm envying is my arthritic friend's patient endurance, maybe I could begin by not shrieking and running around making a fuss about finding the aloe plant when I burn my finger on the iron. Baby steps to begin with; I can't expect myself to start out on the virtuoso heights.

Individuality will inevitably govern the way I organize my priorities, the way each of us must. I have friends whose houses are brightened with graceful touches of handmade work, but crafts are my thing only from time to time. I enjoyed making pot holders during a homemaking meeting: when I look at them (even now, when a corner is singed from being left too close to the burner) I remember a happy, companionable time of chattering with friends and the satisfaction of having completed a project that day. But when I came home, I put the pot holder next to the stove and went back to the things that are more important in the daily fabric of my particular life.

Over and over, I suspect, I'm being taught the same lesson. I am able to learn from people around me, but I am never going to be able to *be* those people. I can't expect myself to be. Other people can suggest directions I might take, but only I can choose which way is the way for me.

It is impossible to go in all the directions people would suggest for us, nor can we get to be good enough at everything all at once. We may not have all the choices we'd like available to us at the same time—sometimes the task that has to be done would be the last one on the list, if we could choose the order—but even if we have choice in nothing else, we always have choice about the attitude we're going to take toward any given situation. I can't really see myself beaming with joy when I'm doing a job I dislike and am doing it simply because it has to be done, but I'm not convinced that's required. Maybe I just have to refrain from moaning about it and feeling sorry for myself.

We said we'd take free agency, and it is both our emancipation and our burden. As self-determining children of our Heavenly Father, we can never be wholly anonymous, enveloped in a crowd. Each of us is separate, with separate gifts and separate challenges. That can be lonely sometimes—even scary. But each of us has the chance to work out the reality of our mortal lives by the choices we make, which will never be precisely the same choices that anyone else has ever made.

Our faces and fingerprints are all different. So are our lives. Some of the expectations we find all around us are universal: for instance, we all must develop patience and kindness and unselfishness and obedience to the commandments. But many expectations—self-generated or originating from outside—are more custom-fitted. We can choose to weave or take up photography or pour our energies into a career or help out with a homeless shelter or have a lithe, well-exercised body or excel in the garden or at the piano.

The commandments we have to work on. But the custom-fitted stuff? That we get to choose, and as we choose, let us remember our motto, cross-stitched or lettered in gold: None of us is ever going to be good enough at everything.

It's a bright thought for a wet Wednesday.

3

On Doing It All

It's not just expectations that create our problems, of course. It wasn't all that long ago that women became fascinated with the tempting mirage of having it all, and started to drive themselves crazy trying to turn the mirage into daily reality.

What "having it all" meant was left conveniently fuzzy, but basically it seemed to boil down to taking on all the interesting things that had been traditionally allocated to men and hanging onto all the things that women had done, as well. It was a mirage born out of enormous hopefulness. Having come to the conclusion that female gender had nothing to do with limits on brain power or basic capability level, women saw themselves as newly empowered, and decided that there was no fundamental reason why they couldn't take a crack at a lot of challenges from which they had been more or less routinely excluded. It was all pretty intoxicating for a while. Maybe it would truly be possible to spread our wings while still sitting on the familiar old nests. Maybe we could explore the new possibilities and still keep on functioning as the "heart of the home." The buzzing was all around us: self-proclaimed experts, glittering role models, media ecstasies—success was obviously at hand.

And then we discovered we were stuck with the same old twenty-four-hour days.

Not all of the revolution in women's roles was born of theoretical premises, however. Like so many social readjustments, the burst of enthusiasm for women's finding more of a role outside their homes was also fueled by less obvious economic realities. Over the last thirty years or so, the United States economy has been shifting from one in which one-income families were the standard to an economy in which, except at the higher end of the income range, it really takes two incomes (or one and a half) to keep a family going, in the traditional sense of being able to buy a house and heat it, put food on the table, and eventually send the kids to college. Depending on whose statistics you use, incomes have been remaining static or even falling in terms of purchasing power. So, women, tantalized by the idea that there might be something out there a whole lot more exciting than there ever had been before, were further motivated into action by discovering that the bills were growing faster than was the single income to pay them.

Which brings us back to the problem of fitting it all in.

Of course, we ordinary housewives, trying to figure out what the new changes meant to our lives, weren't helped much by the fact that a lot of the women doing the most talking were never nest-builders in the first place. There were a lot of differences among the loudest propagandists of revived feminism, but one inescapable motivating element that most of them had in common was sour memories of growing up with a discontented, often bitter mother who chafed at the restrictions of what she (or her daughter) perceived as a narrow, empty life— one in which her only identity was as somebody else's wife or somebody else's mother.

Now, it's perfectly possible to argue quite intelligently that taking that attitude more or less guarantees frustration, but it's not possible to argue that a lot of women do not honestly feel that way, or that revived feminism was not driven mainly by the daughters of some of those discontented women—daughters who were absolutely determined that whatever else happened, they weren't going to find themselves in the same bind. They set their goals in the outside world, they (at least the majority of them) took care not to hamper themselves with permanent relationships or with children, and then they claimed that they had found a brave new world and that so could all the rest of us.

The rest of us found ourselves in a gigantic pothole. "Having it all" (in spite of what the propagandists themselves did in their own private lives) came to mean having a job, having a family, having rewarding intimate relationships (presumably with the family, between washing the socks and producing memorable meals), having an interesting, stimulating personal life, and having all this all at once every single day. What they didn't tell us was that having it all requires somebody to do it all, and that somebody is us, living in a world where fatigue and burnout are not imaginary hurdles.

Undoubtedly there are super-energized women who gobble up demands on their time and thrive on it. However, it is also true that not being one of those women is not a sin—and it's a good thing, since most of us aren't. What most of us discovered, either from trying it out ourselves one way or another or from watching with appalled fascination while other women around us did, is that you can stretch and pull twenty-four hours into any shape you choose, but at the end of the day all you have is twenty-four hours, part of which you have to spend sleeping. We also observed that each of the elements of a life made up of "it all" has its own ebb and flow, which may or more likely may not fit in perfectly with all the other elements. There are, in short, still the wet Wednesdays.

Children get sick at times when the schedule doesn't allow slack for you to cuddle them and spoon-feed soup to them and keep them company when they are convalescent and crabby. The sink is likely to throw a tantrum and spew gunk all over the floor at the least convenient moment. Jobs have their own deadlines and fascinations; there are always the days when it is time to go home but something has to be finished (or you've just reached the fun part and can't bear to stop) in spite of your uncomfortable awareness that several intricate arrangements depend absolutely on your getting home on time. Husbands want and need your undivided attention on evenings when you have an in-service class to attend, grocery shopping that has to be fit in somewhere, and a fifth-grader weeping over long division—and presto, there you are, feeling like it's a wet Wednesday.

Not that it takes things going wrong to upset a perilously balanced apple cart. There isn't even time for the right things, some days. Family activities, personal pleasures—anything that doesn't absolutely *have* to be completed today is too often pushed off to that semimythical moment (next week? next month?) when there will be some time to enjoy whatever it is. And if the last thirteen things that got postponed never happened, maybe this time will be different. And if it isn't—well, even the children have to learn that sometimes what we had hoped for (even something as simple as a family picnic) doesn't quite happen. Gloomily we vow to ourselves that we won't promise so glibly next time, knowing full well that next time we'll be just as hopeful that time will materialize from somewhere and we can do the things we want to do.

"Having it all" sounds terrific, but the cruel twist is that the notion gives us the illusion that we don't have to choose what we're going to accomplish—we'll just do it all—and therefore, since nothing gets eliminated by our making deliberate choices, we hold ourselves accountable for success across the board. Which—surprise, surprise—guarantees failure somewhere along the line, most likely at several somewheres.

The fact is that we do have to choose. It is true that human possibilities are infinitely various, and somewhere there might be a woman who can "do it all" all at once—and if so, she has my awestruck admiration—but the vast majority of us have to choose (and the advice and counsel we are given from the leadership of the Church is based on that reality). When women, wives and mothers, take on additional responsibilities outside the home, the responsibilities inside the home have to be rearranged—and some things won't get done. That is the plain, unvarnished, bottom-line truth, and that's what we have to live with.

As with all deeply personal decisions, only you—and your family—can weigh the various factors and, drawing on prayer and honest evaluation, come up with the final balance. Sometimes we have the luxury of making choices more or less freely, and sometimes circumstances force them on us. For example, if you are a main breadwinner in your family, for whatever reason, devotion of time and energy to earning a living is not optional, and when you have spent that time and energy on the job, they are not available to be spent elsewhere. Maybe it would be nice to have the choice to arrange things otherwise, but if you don't, you don't. And if you don't, there's no point in blaming yourself when, because you are working away from home, there are things you would like to do with the children and can't. That's just the way your particular ball bounces. As a family you'll all have to find compensations for good things that howsoever desirable are not possible.

Not that all paid employment is done outside the home. For Latter-day Saint women, a popular way of supplementing family income is providing day care for the children of other mothers who do have outside jobs, and that arrangement, with its glowing promise of actually earning money and getting to stay at home with your own children while you do it, spawns its own myths about offering an easy way to have it all without having to make the hard choices.

Actually doing day care teaches us otherwise. Anyone who thinks supplying child care at home is not a challenging, exhausting occupation should try it for a couple of weeks. She (or he!) would quickly discover that dealing with the irritating idiosyncrasies of somebody else's child can make you cross with your own; that scooping up a child or two of your own and going to a meeting or the grocery store is routine, but when you have a houseful, you are decidedly housebound; that at the end of the day, when all the other mothers come and collect their offspring, you are likely to be pretty tired yourself, and you still have all the work to do that you couldn't get done with all the children around, and if your husband's coming home, you have some ambitions to be cheerful and attractive instead of tight-lipped and feeling like a frump; and that, perhaps most poignantly, your children have to deal with the daily reality of sharing their mother with other children, who assume they have just as much right to your lap and your attention— and after all, that's exactly what you're being paid to give.

Just like any other job, looking after children has costs, and whereas we certainly have the obligation to try to choose the set of costs that fit in best with our particular circumstances, we can't blame ourselves for the fact that the costs exist. That's just the way life works.

In our brave new world of having it all, even being in the

position to stay at home with your own children has costs. For one thing, there's the annoying tendency of people who should know better to dismiss the daily routine of staying home as mindless emptiness spent talking and thinking on the level of a two-year-old while doing and redoing endless housework— which, as far as it goes, is probably an accurate reflection of some days, but working outside the home is not a continuous round of interest and fascination either.

Still, even people who do what have to be described as repetitious jobs somehow are considered less of a vocational zero than a woman who stays at home. When it comes to children, in many ways our society talks the talk ("Children are vitally important, the hope of our future, and it's absolutely wonderful when an *intelligent* woman chooses to spend her time nurturing her children") but doesn't quite walk the walk ("I work because if I had to stay home all day with the kids, I'd go nuts; beats me how anyone with anything on the ball does it").

It's all very well and good to put your chin up proudly and say that you refuse to go along with trendoids who talk like that. You don't agree with the way they think, the way they talk, or the way they run their own lives, so why pay attention to their opinion of yours? Unfortunately, it's hard to keep your chin up all the time. Even mothers at home have those discouraging days sometimes. Besides, it's very irritating to be considered a vegetable, even a noble one, by people who murmur patronizingly kind words while their eyes drift over your shoulder as they look for somebody interesting to talk to.

Nor is that the only way in which self-esteem suffers. The same rules which mean that a woman who spends time and energy outside the home has less of these to spend inside mean for the housewife that a lot of what she does inevitably takes place privately, unremarked and unappreciated. Unless you have a remarkably attentive and alert husband, nobody really sees what you spend your time and energy on. They don't seem to give out letters of commendation for toilet training with style and without losing your temper too often, nor does anybody say, "Good job!" when you have managed to remove almost all the traces of the red crayon that went through the dryer with the white load. There are no promotions, and whereas jobs in the larger world of work get done and stay done, at home there are always more dishes to be done and beds to be made and dumb questions to be answered. Very likely there are also pennies to be pinched, and for a lot of women, having spells of feeling uninteresting and poor and dowdy is one of the costs of the contemporary choice to stay home.

The most unfortunate aspect of the having-it-all syndrome is that it's managed to produce an emotional climate in which everybody feels defensive, no matter what personal choice was made. We're all challenged either directly or covertly by the different choice that another woman makes.

In my experience, much of the problem is that I have to find real generosity of heart to wholeheartedly approve of somebody who is doing what I have decided I myself ought not to—or cannot—do. For instance, if I'm staying at home because I believe my children will benefit and because we have been counseled to stay home if it is at all possible to do so, it's very hard not to be at least a little judgmental about the women I see all around me who are leaving their children in the care of others while they work, even though I can never know what all went into that decision in the first place. Besides, feeling noble by comparison helps soothe my own longings for the material things we don't have that they might be able to afford, or for the freedom and mental stimulation they may find in getting out of the house and away from the children, who do, in all honesty, test one's patience frequently no matter how much they are loved.

Similarly, a woman who marches off to work every day, knowing she is not sharing the full rhythm of her children's lives—that, if they are little, there are accomplishments such as the first step and the first words that she is likely to miss, or that, if they are bigger, there will be times when they need and want to talk to her and she will simply not be there—finds it hard to be generously accepting, without the defensive kick of guilt, of her neighbor's decision to stay at home, no matter why the woman working outside the home made the decision to maintain paid employment. We all comfort ourselves by looking at the best side of any choice we've made, and if you have to be out working, these comforting aspects may include the spunky independence that your children develop, the interesting parts of what you do during the day (and the knowledge that by staying in the work force, you are gathering experience and seniority that will move you ahead, if you choose), and the little luxuries you might be able to afford when there's more money coming into the household budget. You make a point of remembering a perfectly awful Saturday or a winter school vacation week when you stayed home and everyone was cross and grumpy and you escaped back to the comparative order and sanity of your workplace with genuine relief. It's easier to think about those rough days at home than to remember the good ones, and so the working mothers compare battle stories of life at home, and almost inevitably an edge of thinly veiled contempt creeps in for those poor souls who are stuck at home with their kids *all the time*.

It certainly is odd, isn't it, that what our new freedom of choice seems to have produced, in a practical sense, is that now we all feel guilty no matter what choice we make. You're not good enough either way. The mother at home frets about being less of a person; the mother out at work frets about being less of a woman. As long as each one is pinned by her own emotional necessities, neither one can reach out an uncomplicated hand of sisterhood to the other. Yet goodness knows we all need sisterhood, because quite apart from the employment question, trying to do it all has its challenges.

For one thing, the time pinch usually does little to improve our spiritual lives. Virtue takes time, too. Keeping in touch with Heavenly Father can be done anytime and anywhere, but like a marriage, a relationship with the Lord is unlikely to thrive if all we devote to it are absentminded spare minutes here and there. When we're caught up in the timetable lockstep of an overcrowded life, it's easy to forget that we need more than a few moments of peace if we want to pray effectively. We may need time to listen for our answer—hands might be busy with some routine task (folding the laundry, maybe, or even driving the car), but the spirit has to have enough serenity to be receptive, and peace and serenity tend to be thin on the ground when you're trying to cram a quart's worth of activity into a pint pot of time.

Sometimes one of the paths to that peace and serenity is to look at what can and cannot reasonably be done. Too often we feel like failures because, as part of the "all," we're taking on responsibilities that were never ours, and never can be.

For our worthy ancestors, life may have been hard, but at least it was simpler. My great-grandmother and my triple-great-grandmother had their problems, but I suspect their main concerns were with the practical matters of keeping their families housed and clothed and fed. We assume that those are also our responsibilities today, but coming from our end of this psychologically oriented century, we also have come to believe that we all should be well adjusted (which we translate as meaning "happy") while we're carrying out those responsibilities; and we seem to believe that, if we do it right, it's possible to make sure that everyone around us whom we love and who is in our charge is well-adjusted—which is to say, "happy"—too. Achieving that, the expectations of the world seem to whisper, is the minimum requirement of doing it all, whatever that "all" happens to mean to any one of us.

So we fuss and we fret over our children's adjustment to school and to each other and to the incipient bully down the block—along with worrying and praying over their development of testimonies of their own—and if there are times when life isn't turning out to be a golden glide for them, we wonder nervously if it's all our fault. Or maybe our concern is a husband who's having a bleak patch, and we feel that somehow we should be able to cushion it for him—make him feel better, even though logically we know it's the work situation that's getting on top of him. Or maybe Mother is growing into mobility problems which wreak havoc on her morale, and we take that on our own shoulders, too—after all, she's *Mother*—and as her self-esteem sinks, ours goes right along as well, because we couldn't figure out how to make her happier.

Trying to be conscientious about our responsibilities, we find it doesn't make a lot of difference whether we're away at work, gnawing away at those problems as we walk between rows of desks, or at home, absentmindedly wiping the counters while we go back and forth over the same discouraging ground in our thoughts. Wherever we are, we have to find the point of equilibrium between intelligent self-interest and unselfishness, and above all, we have to remember the principles of individual responsibility and free agency.

We may tell ourselves, if we're in the workforce, that all this wouldn't be happening if we were home; or, if we're at home, we may assume that since we're around all the time we should be able to solve whatever it is, if we are worthy enough. Unfortunately, going at the problem from either of those angles leads straight to the trap of believing that we have the power to take control of somebody else's life. However much we love them, those people are themselves and not extensions of us. Some of us do have children or husbands (or parents or siblings, as far as that goes) who do face greater-than-average hurdles of psychological adjustment, but some of us have family members with physical handicaps, too, and just as we can't by the force of our willpower bring sight to a blind child or sound to a deaf one, so we can't wave a wand and magic unhappiness away. We can't even eliminate the absolutely normal downs that interrupt the ups of life. Consider the wet Wednesdays!

What is absolutely certain is that there is no way we can assume ownership of anybody else's problems. We can help, we can support, we can encourage, but we cannot do anybody else's job of living for them. Whatever "all" we might be trying to do, solving other people's problems for them cannot, and must not, be part of it.

As many worldly but wise philosophers have pointed out, you play the game with the hand dealt to you. The cards are what they are—your accomplishment lies in what you do with them. The point at which many of us go off the track is when we somehow expect that we ought to have all fifty-two cards in the deck available to us simultaneously and continuously, and there is no game known to mortal man (or woman) in which that is true.

Often, when we are feeling overwhelmed, all we really need is the reassurance that there is more to the year of life than the season we can see outside the window right now. Time passes, and circumstances change. People dear to us—and we ourselves—move through all the fluctuations of moods. Children grow in and out of stages; adults find that their own lives modulate from one kind of stress to another, and some kinds are easier to cope with than others.

What we can be sure of is that little children grow up, and as they do so, our daily burden of responsibility to them lessens. For some women this means that the homebound years open out to greater freedom to explore the world beyond their neighborhood, and maybe even the challenge of trying paid employment. For others, who have spent years out in that often inhospitable world, the daunting financial burden eases off as children move into independence, and there is not such urgency in having to have that paycheck (and every penny of it, too). One of the presents one woman might be able to afford for herself is more time, even if it means not quite so much money coming in—time, maybe, to do some of the at-home things that a sister who is tentatively exploring the wider world is so joyfully escaping after all the years of having her immediate neighborhood mark the boundaries.

Of course, few of us are discontented most of the time, and there are some who seem to be gifted with serenity and who apparently absorb by osmosis the lessons that the rest of us struggle to learn. Still, it is good sometimes to make a point of remembering that our circumstances do not define us and that, in any case, the only constant is change. Having it all is a splendid ambition, as long as we are willing to give ourselves the span of a lifetime to fit it all in.

It seems that at times we find it curiously difficult to trust in the Lord. Remember Peter, who stepped out on the water but then wavered, despite the fact that the Savior had beckoned him and was near? Perhaps sometimes we are like that about our lives. If we don't have it now, we're afraid we never will have it. The Lord is more generous than that. What we need to make sure of is that we don't disregard the pleasures of now in worrying about when we will move on to later. Later will come, in later's good time—and it would be a pity to spend the future looking back with yearning for what we right now are so busy trying to escape that we cannot enjoy it.

No single day is long enough to crowd in all the blessings our Heavenly Father has in store for us. Having it all will usually mean, as it must, having bits of it—day after day after day.

4

On Beating the Competition

Different we're bound to be. So why do we spend so much time checking over our shoulders to see how everybody else is doing?

It drives me crazy when my children do it. Take an average Sunday, for example. The family is milling around, on the way out the door to get into the car. I comment to my older daughter how nice she looks this morning, and her sister darkens like a thunderstorm. "What's wrong with my dress?" she quavers. It's most exasperating.

It doesn't occur to me, of course, that exactly the same mechanism is in effect when I come home from attending a women's conference class on gardening and stand gloomily surveying my own backyard (observe untidy borders, interesting outgrowths of persistent weeds, tomato plants that are doing their best to sprawl over to the lawn). I am washed by the old familiar wave of guilt and inadequacy, because I never have been a gardener and apparently never will be a gardener, but if I had my act together at least I could keep the place looking a little more like the good sister's who taught the class, and the fact that I don't is one more proof that I *don't* have my act together, et cetera, et cetera. The only thing missing for a precise parallel between my daughter and me is my wailing, "What's wrong with me?"

Nor is it only gardening, of course. I am just as envious and defensive about a number of other practical and decorative skills, time management practices, housekeeping efficiency—really, when I think about it, my first impulse is to ask whether you want the short list or the long list of what other people do better than I do. The only thing that keeps me from concluding that I am coping with an aggravated case of personal paranoia is the clear memory of complimenting another woman on something she has done (an exquisite piece of cross-stitching, for example, or maybe a crisply fresh stenciled border around kitchen cabinets), only to have the woman in question laugh self-consciously and say, "Oh, I just followed the directions. You should see what Ruthelma does, and *she* does it all out of her own head. *She's* wonderful."

Now, is that an appropriate sense of modesty, the generosity of sisterhood, or an unconscious reflection of the belief that it only really counts if you are not only good at something but also the best one around at whatever it is? Clearly, modesty or generosity are no problem—we can use all of either that we can find available—but I'm afraid that too often it's that hidden unacknowledged competitiveness that not only robs us of feeling comfortable about accepting any compliments but even prevents us from feeling good inside ourselves about what we've done. After all, if what we see when we look at our own handiwork is only how much more colorful and elaborate somebody else's is, doesn't some of our justified satisfaction in completing the project drain sadly away?

We live in a very competitive society, accustomed to ranking almost any accomplishment as good, better, or best. In so many fields success is the business of doing better than the next guy. The product that's successful sells more units than the competing brand. The store that's successful has more customers than the one next door. The runner who's successful runs faster than the runner in the next lane. It's hardly surprising that we tend to internalize and transfer the attitude that for something to be good it has to be better than something else, and that we live at least part of the time checking nervously on how everyone else is doing.

I remember that in my growing-up years, when I was lamenting the fact that somebody or other had more of something than I did, my mother would say matter-of-factly, "There will always be people who have more than you, and there will always be people who have less." At the time I thought she was rather hard-hearted, refusing to sympathize with me, but I have come to appreciate that she was simply being realistic. I have also come to discover that the permanent existence of people who have more and people who have less doesn't apply only to possessions. It is equally applicable to talents and skills, which means that when I look out of the corner of my eye to check on how the competition is doing, I sometimes discover I'm keeping up or ahead, and rather more often I discover the competition's out ahead of me.

There's no difficulty when I'm the one who's excelling. I think we all can handle that with suitable if not entirely genuine modesty. What gets to be more challenging is responding with grace (internal as well as external) when the fact is that I am being well and truly outdone. The challenge doesn't lessen when what I'm measuring myself against is not a straightforward matter of competence (producing needlepoint Christmas stockings for the whole family, say, or maybe making the most felicitous choice of new wallpaper to fit in with the old) but a question of virtue, something that I hope to take forward with me into eternity: my success (or lack of it), say, in being a person, a mother, a wife—whatever.

The problem with that, however, is a basic one. With some enterprises, how someone else is doing may be measurable, but when it comes to my efforts to acquire virtue—being a person trying to become a better person—comparison is wholly irrelevant. Not only that, but since in any case it is highly unlikely that I can be better at everything everyone around me tries to do, the exercise of comparison is more likely to be depressing than anything else.

One of the elementary difficulties in transferring the competitive lessons of the outside world to the patterns of our personal lives is that whereas competence is often well adapted for comparative evaluation, virtue isn't. Salesmen, to take an obvious example, can be easily ranked by their competence as more successful or less successful. There's an available, applicable yardstick: How much did they sell? How much more than the average? How much more than the next most successful? And so on. You can wind up with a neat, unambiguous ranking: good, better, and, solitary at the top, best.

But where's the yardstick for friends? wives? mothers? Oh, I suppose there's a basic minimum level of behavior that we all assume as being adequate, even if we don't often define it: after all, treacherous friends, irresponsible wives, and uncaring mothers do exist. But once you've reached the threshold of adequate, what on earth (literally) do better and best mean? How can I or anyone else, short of the Lord, evaluate whether my sister worker in Primary or my neighbor next door are better mothers than I am? They have different children and different challenges than I do, and there is no earthly measuring unit on a yardstick to compare how each of us is succeeding. We can't even use how the children turn out as a reliable long-term rating scale: kids aren't products of their parents' influence and efforts alone. It's true that we were told that by their fruits we shall know them, but the Lord was talking about other enterprises (see Matthew 7:20). Fruit—even metaphorical fruit—doesn't have free agency. Children do. I don't suppose there is a mother alive who hasn't at one time or another earnestly wished that her children would be a more predictable gauge of the colossal effort she's putting into mothering them, but they just plain aren't. The single consolation (perhaps not a wholly charitable one) is that her children's children won't be predictable, either.

If you can't make a valid comparative scale on mothering, how about "wife-ing"? Fast Sunday after fast Sunday we hear our good brothers stand and declare that they each have the best wife in the world, but can that possibly mean anything more than a public declaration of husbandly devotion? Best wife—best at what? And according to whose rating scale? Her husband's or my husband's or husbands' in general?

Nor is friendship more quantifiable and comparable. When we were little, we had best friends, and even now there is often one person whose needs and enjoyments interlock comfortably with our own—a situation we often appreciate most, sadly, when one or the other of us has to move away. But what makes a friend "best" to me wouldn't necessarily work for anyone else.

There are people extraordinarily gifted in friendship, but their gifts aren't the kind that can be tallied up and measured against another person's. The gift of friendship itself is the ability to make each relationship individual and unique. In fact, part of what makes a best friend feel so comfortable and cozy is exactly that uniqueness—the recognition that the two of you do share something (maybe the same things make you giggle, or you could both spend hours in companionable antiquing) that you don't share with everyone else you know. There isn't a measuring stick for that kind of thing, any more than there is one for wife-ing or mothering. There's no race; there's no one to beat.

But if human relationships are nonquantifiable and noncomparable, I argue with myself, isn't there still something to be said for using the examples of those around me to hone my own aspirations, to give me specific areas to work on being better at? Isn't competition a good motivator? Why not measure how far you're getting by comparing your progress with that of other people trying to do the same things you are?

Well, wait, the other voice in my head answers—the less impatient, more thoughtful voice. Maybe what we're looking at here is the old question of ends and means.

The trouble with using competition to spur us on in our personal development is that an inevitable part of competition is beating somebody else out. You can't be better, competitively, unless somebody else is worse. What makes the winner in a spelling bee is that everybody else failed. You can't win a race unless somebody else loses. The competitive goal is to be standing triumphant on the top of the heap of everybody else who didn't make it: one winner and a whole lot of losers, and the greater the number of losers, the greater the triumph of the win. Competition is inherently selfish. Competence may be the measuring rod, but it's pride that goads us on.

Which is not to say that what we all ought to do is retire to some isolated commune and attempt to shuck off all competitive challenges on the spot. Competition is a here-and-now aspect of our here-and-now world. If there is anything that our Church history (and now world history) has taught us over the last century or so, it's that at this stage in our development, competition is a powerful motivator, and given the spur of competition, a lot of things get done that don't seem to happen unless people are competing with each other. The united order, which would have replaced competition with cooperation, had limited success: many Saints simply weren't dedicated and unselfish enough for those united-order communities to function as they were planned.

Communism, too, specifically rejected the principle of competition, and communism didn't work. Whether it didn't work because it also denied free agency, or whether it didn't work because it put primary emphasis on the community and not on the individual, or whether it didn't work because it depended on people working hard whether or not there was any particular reward for working hard is probably something that will keep political scientists cogitating and arguing for the next couple of centuries. But, demonstrably, it *didn't* work, and nation after nation is turning to free enterprise, with the spur of competition, to get their societies going again. So there seems to be a space, in the here and now, for competition.

Of course, we are here-and-now creatures. In part, that's what we came to this earth to experience. But we are also more, and it's in our relationships with others and, perhaps even more important, in our most private assessment of ourselves that we have to take that "more" into account. We are trying to refine ourselves. We are trying to be more of what we have to be if this earth step is to be what it's meant to be: an opportunity to learn to make choices, and to grow.

Maybe what we need to work on, instead of always struggling to be the better one, is developing a greater generosity of spirit, an orientation that will allow us to work on our own accomplishments and genuinely delight in the accomplishments of others—and not get the two things mixed up, which is harder than it looks.

It seems curious, but concentration helps. It helps in two ways. When you're working on your own project, concentration helps block out some of the ground clutter—the temptation to look around and compare how you're coming with how everybody who's near you is doing. Succumbing to that temptation seems to be one of the things that is virtually guaranteed to tumble me into one of those discouraging days.

I know logically what the antidote is. If I can manage to keep my attention on what I'm trying to do, I can't worry about whether it looks kind of pathetic next to somebody else's. Say I'm undertaking bread making. Quite honestly, I'm not one of those who does it routinely on a weekly basis. This means that there's always a certain element of hopefulness in my anticipation that it will turn out well this time. If I concentrate on what I'm doing, instead of thinking about all those fat, picture-perfect loaves that Georgia-down-the-street regularly produces, and keep my mind on the smooth elastic feel of the yeasty dough and the satisfactory thumping of kneading (you can work off a lot of steam on a ball of dough) and the absolutely wonderful smell of bread baking—well, Georgia's loaves become a lot less important to me. After all, my kitchen smells just as good as hers, even if what I produce are smaller, determined-looking, stumpy loaves. Besides, even bread with texture that leaves something to be desired tastes good.

Then, if I happen to stop in at Georgia's, and if I can keep my mind on paying attention to *her* bread-making skills (instead of wistfully bemoaning my stumpy loaves when I look at her fat ones), in the first place, I might pick up some useful information, and in the second place, instead of focusing forlornly on her skill and my lack of it—which inevitably makes a barrier between the two of us—substituting generosity for competition means that we can both share in enjoying what she obviously does so well.

The reward, if we do manage to step past competitiveness and open ourselves to that generosity, is that it feels terrific. For one thing, it means abandoning an immense burden of pressure. The hard part is unclenching your fingers from the competitive challenge in the beginning, persuading yourself consciously that you can admire what someone else does, or has, or is capable of, without feeling that you ought to do it, or have it, or be similarly capable yourself. You can just relax and purely enjoy what's going on, like an oversized Victorian lady suddenly free of her corset.

Maybe the first step in that direction is teaching ourselves to enjoy the skills of others in fields where we genuinely don't care whether we're any good or not. For me, perhaps, one of those fields might be tennis. Long ago I gave up the hope that I would ever be any good at it. Very occasionally I have been talked into getting a racket and panting around the court for a while, but I have to say what I enjoy most is the chatter back and forth across the net (clearly I do not play at the high-pressure level) and having something cold to drink afterwards. And yet I have to admit that watching tennis being played well, even by amateurs down at the park, is enjoyable. Maybe I can begin teaching myself generosity of spirit by watching my friends play without allowing myself the selfishness of mentally lamenting that I don't have their quickness, or grace, or even just basic skills that have taken hours of practice to acquire. Maybe I can just share the pleasure of what's going on and retrieve runaway balls, if that helps. Maybe that way I can start to learn to let go of envy and jealousy and competitiveness, and purely and simply enjoy what they do well. After all, tennis isn't really my thing. And then when I go home, I can work on my own skills—knitting, or writing, or something else that is important to me—without conscious reference to anyone else at all.

And if I begin to master that first step, maybe I can go on to learn to admire as spontaneously and generously the skills that I do really want to have, without secretly and jealously comparing my own skills to those of others. Maybe I can even come to enjoy the beautiful front yard of the good sister who taught the gardening class, without giving a thought to the condition of my own. Maybe, freed by generosity, I can even take some inspiration home, instead of the old wash of inadequacy, and do something about my own backyard, without trying to catch up to hers or anybody else's. (But I could borrow some of her ideas about bulbs.)

Maybe I can overhear, and admire, a friend's particularly deft handling of an adolescent tempest in a teacup, without feeling the stroke of guilt that I made a real hash the last time I was similarly placed. Maybe I can relax and enjoy a visit in a spotless house without seeing its existence as a commentary on my own housekeeping. After all, our mortal existence is not a footrace with a finishing line and a scoreboard to register first, second, third, and also-ran. When we are really evaluating our progress, we have to get beyond the competitive, earthbound mind-set to something closer to our Father's point of view.

It is quite true that while we're here on earth some of us are always going to be better than others at some things; some of us (the very same ones, in fact) are going to be worse at other things. In the here and now we can't all win all the races. One of the things we all have to teach our children is that winning is fun but that sometimes you lose. Our time and effort are finite, and we have to choose where we spend either one. In my garden of here and now—even in that good sister's far more beautiful garden—things get crowded out. Not everything fits. You can't plant both peonies and Shasta daisies in precisely the same spot. If you try (and I have) one will "win": one grows and the other doesn't. It's not only people that compete.

But our Father's garden is generous, expansive, and infinite. There is room for all of us, and provision for all of us to succeed. Nobody else, no matter how well they do whatever they do, can take over my place. Nor can I (even should I suddenly be translated to magnificence) spread over and usurp somebody else's. Each of us has been placed so that we can grow and flourish, and so what happens subsequently is in our own power to control.

There is room for us all. There always has been, and there always will be—and that, after all, is one of the many differences between an earthbound perspective and the eternal. It may even be that as we manage to wriggle loose from some of the competitive acquisitiveness that belongs to this earthly perspective, we might get a glimpse of the freedom stretching out beyond it.

Eternity has plenty of time for generosity. We may even have some time for it now.

5

On Esteeming a Self

Would it make wet Wednesdays easier if we each had indestructible, guaranteed-to-bounce-back self-esteem?

Maybe. Maybe not. I can't help but suspect that this might not be the whole solution for everybody: I know the reasons for my discouraging days often have a lot to do with external conditions as well (the ups and downs of relating to other people, budgetary difficulties, the length of the day versus the time inevitably consumed by the things I need to accomplish during it, and so on). But perhaps all the pop psychologists and self-help manuals have a point—that none of the above would bother me as much as long as my self-esteem was right up there.

It would be nice if self-esteem could insulate us from discouragement. Who wouldn't like to feel comfortable about herself all the time, never hesitating or worrying about saying the wrong thing, and being able to handle whatever situation life dumps in her lap? To be sure enough of your own acceptability to launch confidently into the party instead of hanging back tentatively at the doorway as you hunt hopefully for a familiar face; to be sure enough of yourself that ordinary setbacks aren't unduly discouraging and criticism can be taken with aplomb; to be sure enough to be able to risk trying new experiences without being cramped by the memory of the past ones that didn't come out right—what could be more agreeable?

Certainly we hear enough about self-esteem. Experts, qualified and self-proclaimed, discuss its importance; our children's teachers plan projects to enhance it; our classes in Relief Society emphasize it. It would be tempting to declare resoundingly that developing healthy self-esteem is *the* critical goal, until we remember that what's critical about it is that it's an essential starting block. It's not the ultimate destination.

Quite simply, the greatest advantage of self-esteem is that it frees you from turning inward, fretting about yourself, and enables you to take your own state of being for granted—in a comfortable way—and get on with something else. The something else might well be self-improvement: a sound sense of self-esteem doesn't mean you are as good as you can become. But if you are plagued with an inability to believe in your own capacities right now, it's going to be very hard to make much headway on the job of improving any of them, just as it's hard for a little kid to concentrate on learning to tie his shoelaces if he's uncertain about how to put the shoe on in the first place.

There's been enough talk about self-esteem that a lot of people have a lot of different ways of describing it, but most of the definitions seem to boil down to an agreement that self-esteem encompasses both confidence in your ability to do things and confidence that you have value in and of yourself. On the one hand, you need to feel that you are personally competent: not necessarily the best one in the world at whatever you do, but good enough to get the job done and provide yourself with some satisfaction from having done it. On the other, you need to feel a sense of personal worth: that there's more to you than being somebody's daughter, or somebody's wife, or somebody's mother—that somewhere, underneath and connecting all those roles, is a person in her own right, a person who counts.

It seems simple enough. When we look at our kids, we can see the way it works (or the way it ought to work) quite clearly. Now, they may be our kids, but we know they've got the potential to do just about anything they set their minds to, and we want them to know it, too, even when at exactly the same mo-

ment we're haranguing them about elbows on the table or failure to get serious about homework completion or being unnec-
essarily critical of each other. Even given those imperfections
(and all the others that come immediately to mind), we have
absolute confidence in their abilities, if they'll just straighten up
and get organized. So why is it so much harder to believe in our
own abilities?

Part of the problem, I suspect, comes from the fact that
most of us get uneasy when we try to focus on our own skills
and our own virtues. We've been taught not to brag, not to
toot our own horns, and it feels wrong to draw attention, even
our own, to our achievements. It feels much more righteous to
contemplate our shortcomings. Besides, who knows better than
we do the limits of those achievements—the messy edges, the
grand design we started out with that got cut back along the
way? And (the most daunting thought), would anybody else
consider it such an achievement anyway? Everybody else probably does that kind of thing three times before breakfast.

The thing is, of course, that what anybody else does or
doesn't do, admires or doesn't admire, shouldn't really have
anything to do with self-esteem anyway. Self-esteem, as the
name itself points out, doesn't have a lot to do with anybody
else—except to the extent we let it. Like those painful revela-
tions on the scales in the humid privacy of the bathroom, self-
esteem is strictly a one-on-one business—me and myself. It's
the most informed assessment of my life, made by the person
who knows me inside out. Ideally that assessment should be
dispassionately honest, seeing the good points and the
strengths with the same clarity as the stupidities and the weaknesses—but just the idea of looking at ourselves with that kind
of attention makes a lot of us feel a little queasy.

Why on earth should that be so? The most obvious answer
is probably the right one: because we're afraid of what we'll see.
It's just easier to stick the whole problem furtively in the back
of our minds, the way we stick that unidentified key kicking
around the kitchen into the miscellaneous drawer. Someday
we'll find the time to figure the whole thing out, and in the
meantime we'll move on to something else.

If that's what we do to avoid confronting ourselves, it's a
very womanly course of action—at least, if you take "womanly"

to apply to the observed reality of the way a lot of women be-
have, as opposed to their potential. Women as a whole (and
sadly, this applies to women in the Church, too) appear to be
quick to believe that their accomplishments don't add up to all
that much. They are just as quick to be apologetic about the
ways they fall short of what they apparently assume the world
expects of them.

We don't start out like that. The new rush of studies search-
ing out the differences between male and female reports over-
whelmingly that little girls are very much like little boys in their
headlong, open enthusiasm for trying the world out. They learn
as quickly—in fact, in terms of verbal comprehension, young
girls outdo young boys, and are right up there with them when
it comes to mathematical aptitude. The odd thing is that when
we girls get to be about twelve and thirteen, our measured abilities sag, and the boys surge out ahead and stay there. In a very
parallel manner (and who is to say which causes which?) our
self-esteem plummets, and we are more likely to grow up being
somewhat hesitant, apologetic, and self-effacing.

What happens? There is no shortage of theories, many of
which cast more light on the theorist than on the conclusions.
There are those who hold that it's the result of girls' recognizing that it's a male-dominated world and that female success is
likelier if a girl concentrates more on charming the boys and
being taken under their protection than on trying to keep up.
According to this theory, a girl bright enough to excel is bright
enough to observe that men do not appreciate being outdone,
but if she then chooses to hang back to let the boys around her
succeed, the price of her decision to withdraw from competition is too often the loss of her confidence in her ability to
compete or in her abilities in general.

There are those who believe that the subtle sexist discrimi-
nation of teachers makes the difference. Some studies show that
boys are often pushed harder and that their progress is more
uniformly supervised. Whether or not the girls succeed is presumably assumed to be less important, and so they, consequently, are more likely to drift away from trying to excel. It's
not difficult to see that a girl in such a situation could conclude
that it's not so much her schoolwork that's less important as it

is that she herself is—not precisely the conclusion that leads to sturdy self-esteem.

Then there are those who maintain that it's all biological and that the cultural factors simply underline the inevitable differences of abilities and attitudes. However, since that line of argument includes significant limits on free agency, it's not very useful for our perception of reality. There clearly are differences between men and women, but there is nothing in those differences to determine that well-developed self-esteem is a male prerogative. There are (and always have been) strong, confident women in the Church—a comforting fact to hang on to when we are feeling less than strong and confident ourselves.

As a practical matter, however, the debate between the experts' theories of why many women suffer from low self-esteem is less likely to help us figure out how to improve things than simply deciding that even if our self-esteem sagged along with our achievements back when we were in junior high, that's no reason why we have to live with the sag now. (Nor, in passing, is there any reason why we should overlook the possibility that our daughters' self-images might need some particular attention from us around that time.) Contemplating these theories of how women may or may not be shortchanged by society may be interesting, but it isn't particularly useful in trying to figure out what to do about self-esteem that languishes a thought or two this side of self-confidence, mainly because these theories encourage us to place the responsibility for how our lives develop on somebody else's shoulders—and a mighty nebulous somebody at that.

So, of course, does blaming our parents for the way we feel about ourselves now. It is an observable fact that all parents make mistakes, sometimes unimportant ones and sometimes some major ones. It is also an observable fact that children, even after they've grown up and are no longer in physical childhood, tend to remember at least some of these mistakes. We may not always have accurate recall, true, but we think we remember, we resolve to be perfect parents in our turn, and we fail from time to time as well, sometimes in the same ways as our parents and sometimes by trying to do exactly the opposite. Most of us, like most of our parents, are genuinely trying to do the best we can, and most of our mistakes can be chalked up as good intentioned and will be good preparation for our children, who will grow up to live in a world of fallible people.

A problem arises, however, when some of the mistakes hack away at the emerging self-esteem of a child. Sometimes the mistakes come from overzealousness to help the child improve, the classic case being that of the parent who, seeing the child's report card with all A's and a single B, demands to know why the B. Sometimes the mistakes come out of the parent's own fear that the world is disappointing and that the child should be prepared for failure. Sometimes it's hard to figure out what's going on in a parent's head. Maybe their own self-confidence is so low that they absolutely honestly cannot conceive that a child of theirs might succeed, and so they only comment on the traits that confirm their own vision of reality. Still, however it comes about, there can be significant damage, and if you happen to be the person who was damaged, the most obvious remedy, once you have come to realize what happened, is to point an accusing finger.

The problem with that, in the first place, is that a finger pointed accusingly doesn't do much to help the parent and doesn't do much to help you. Blaming somebody else may be temporarily emotionally satisfying, but it doesn't do much to rectify the damage. After all, what we are taught over and over, in hundreds of varying contexts, is that what happens to you is not what's important; it's what you do about it. What you need to do about it boils down to basically what anybody else with self-esteem dragging in the dust has to do: you take responsibility for yourself as a beloved child of our Heavenly Father and start building on your strengths instead of picking at your weaknesses.

The fact is that we all have strengths. Not one single one of us was sent here to this earth giftless. Unfortunately, a lot of us have much better vision when it comes to identifying the strengths of others than we have when we look at ourselves—or maybe we are inclined to discount our own abilities, believing that the only talents that count are the ones that show off well in public. Maybe we just conclude that the ordinary daily run of life doesn't offer us much scope for developing whatever abilities we have. Do we pay enough attention to the kind of competence that makes even ordinary life more rewarding?

In her autobiography, mystery writer Agatha Christie wrote with affection about her father. She said proudly that he was an *agreeable* man. She wrote: "He had no outstanding characteristics. He was not particularly intelligent. I think that he had a simple and loving heart, and he really cared for his fellow men. . . . There was no meanness in him, no jealousy, and he was almost fantastically generous. And he had a natural happiness and serenity." Consequently, the people who came in contact with him, she said, enjoyed a great measure of happiness themselves. (See *An Autobiography* [New York: Bantam Books, 1977], pp. 3–4.)

Maybe we don't pay enough attention to agreeableness now, but the people who are lucky enough to live with agreeability know its rewards. Still, how many comfortable, easygoing women ever give themselves credit for their agreeability as one of their great strengths?

Or how about the ability to wade into the middle of a quarrel between offspring and to engineer something like justice and at least a temporary truce? I remember talking to a cousin of mine who had gone out to work in a social agency after many years at home with her four children. She wasn't entirely sure of what skills she could bring to the workplace, but she discovered she was very good at one thing without thinking about it: she had become an accomplished peacemaker.

"It turns out that I am very skilled in mediation and conflict resolution," she said ruefully. "I would have said that as a joke five years ago, but being in my job, it's no joke. I need to be a good mediator, and luckily, I discovered I have immense skills in the area of mediation—and that's from having four kids who didn't always get along." Most of us who are in the business of teaching families to live together in something approaching harmony are doing daily in-service training on conflict resolution and mediation, although we might not think of it that way. Those are skills the wider world needs desperately, and yet do we count them among our strengths?

Working out priorities is another skill that's in high demand and that women managing families develop as a matter of course.

We don't usually think of giving ourselves credit for our adeptness in balancing the requirements of running a household (with all the picky little details that that involves). How often do we congratulate ourselves for coping as the singular mother of plural children, each of whom feels entitled to our undivided attention when it seems necessary, not to mention a husband who assumes his wife will automatically focus on him when he has something to tell her or share with her? That's common, run-of-the-mill stuff, we would say if we thought about it. Usually we don't.

We don't even blink when our responsibilities at church, and probably some community involvement, get tossed in. Oh, we may have weeks when we feel kind of overwhelmed by it all, but we are slow to notice the complexity of the weeks in between, when things run routinely and we shuttle back and forth smoothly from one demand to the next, working out priorities that shift and re-form from day to day. Our families may take it all as much for granted as we do, but those skills are precisely the ones that are increasingly valued in government and industry in our increasingly complicated world. Shouldn't we also value that competence in ourselves?

There are dozens of other ordinary gifts and talents that make the ups and downs of ordinary life more enjoyable or more comfortable or just more interesting. We usually see them when they belong to somebody else, but we're curiously blind about ourselves. It has been said that the need is for us to be tough with ourselves and tender with others. This suggestion may have its merits, but as we struggle to maintain a healthy self-esteem we should consider applying some of that tenderness to ourselves. Maybe we should start by looking as favorably at our own strengths as we do at the strengths of others.

The same thing could be said about coming to terms with our weaknesses and with what can be done about them. If we had a good friend come to us and sigh hopelessly, "I'm lazy, that's what's wrong with me, I'm just plain lazy," how many of us would snap back promptly, "Yes, you're quite right. You are lazy, and being lazy is a terrible way to be. I can't imagine how you can go on like that, not getting things done and just wasting time. I don't understand why you don't get a grip on yourself and your life and actually get things done the way you

know you should. Haven't you got any self-discipline at all?"
And yet isn't that just the sort of thing that we're inclined to
mutter to ourselves in the privacy of our own minds?

But to our friend we're more likely to murmur comfort-
ingly, "Oh, you're not lazy. What's so lazy, anyway? Every time
I see you you're on the move."

And the friend would probably say something like, "Well,
I've been meaning to get to clearing out my basement for three
weeks now, and it's even worse now than it was when I decided
something simply had to be done. Every morning I resolve that
today will be the day, and then I put it off and put it off and
find other stuff that needs doing, and then it's too late and I
give up and go to bed."

Whereupon you say, "Oh, for heaven's sake, you're not
lazy. You just don't want to clean up your basement. I hate
that, too," and the conversation drifts on easily to something
else. Maybe you even offer to come on over and help, on the
principle that yucky jobs go better with two at work on them.

In the case of your friend, you could see easily that general-
izing about her essential nature on the basis of a particular action (or lack of action) was unreasonable. But with ourselves?
We leap effortlessly from the particular (you forgot about your
son's T-ball practice) to the general (you are an irresponsible
person). And the trouble with that, aside from the fact that it is
depressing, is that blaming yourself for generalized irresponsibility more or less precludes your taking any action on what the
problem really is. In the case of the forgotten practice, what
you probably need to do is spend less time castigating yourself
for irresponsibility and more time writing things down on the
calendar and then putting the calendar where you can't avoid
looking at it.

After all, improving self-esteem doesn't mean overlooking
the fact that we all have genuine shortcomings. We do. If we
didn't, we wouldn't have much to learn here on this earth. But
when we blow individual actions up into monstrous character
defects, we prevent ourselves from achieving the satisfaction—
and consequent lift in general self-esteem level—of coming to
terms with a shortcoming and overcoming it. As long as I'm accusing myself of irresponsibility, or laziness, or selfishness, or
stupidity, there's no place to start. What I need to determine is

what I did that was irresponsible, or lazy, or selfish, or stupid. Only then am I in a position to take any specific action to improve the situation, and this, unless I really believe an unseen hand is going to reorganize my life, is the only way anything is ever going to improve. And once we have gotten a grip on something we know needs changing, and we have changed it, we can't help but look at that same old face in the mirror with new respect; and it's out of that shyly unfolding self-respect that a healthier sense of self-esteem grows.

There are voices out in the world that suggest that what we need to do to improve our self-esteem is to look at ourselves with greater love and understanding and to accept what we see. For us, working within the framework of the gospel, those voices are speaking only part of the truth. Yes, we need to look at ourselves with greater love and understanding, because that is the way our Heavenly Father looks at us (and the way we look at our own children). On the other hand, we can look at a daughter who insists solemnly that she never touched the cookies (the crumbs all around her mouth as she speaks) and love and understand her perfectly—a plate of fragrantly fresh cookies is a terrible temptation for a little girl—and accept her as she is, and still know that she has to be taught not only that you don't take things that don't belong to you but also that you tell the truth. Acceptance, like self-esteem itself, is only a starting point. It's not the destination.

When we embrace the gospel, we also accept the challenge that Christ gave during his ministry on earth: "Be ye therefore perfect, even as your Father which is in heaven is perfect" (Matthew 5:48). We know we aren't perfect now, and we know we should be working to become so. If self-esteem meant only self-acceptance, what would the call to perfection mean?

And what about humility? It isn't a very popular virtue these days. You don't see magazine articles about humility, and I've never heard a talk show host, on television or radio, discussing the place of humility in our lives. The few times I've heard the word used outside of Church contexts, it's been in connection with either a joke or a genteel sneer. But the scriptures speak highly of it, and when we are closest to the Lord—in the temple, or caught up in one of those prayers where we

really have the certain knowledge that we are speaking to the
Lord and we feel his love and his inspiration wrapping around
us—humility seems the only appropriate response. To insist on
the integrity and value of our selfness at those moments seems
not only impertinent but unnecessary.

What is so striking about those moments, in fact, is that we
become unconscious of ourselves as separate from our Father in
Heaven, and much of our joy comes from the very sense of
being united with him—of moving out and beyond our own
selfness, esteemed or not. And once we've felt that, we know
with absolute certainty that that is the direction in which we
must be moving if we are going to return to his presence. So
what about self, and self-esteem, then?

Perhaps the worldly concept and definition of self-esteem
can carry us only so far. Maybe what we need to do is to turn
the concept of self-esteem in our hands and look at it from another direction. Maybe what we should mean by *self-esteem* is
not so much a sense of satisfaction and acceptance of where we
stand now as a recognition that wherever we are, no matter
how ham-handed and inefficient and unfortunately prone to
making stupid mistakes we might be, we nonetheless each, individually, hold the potential to reach perfection. We hold the potential not only to be able to return to our Father's presence
but also to feel wholly at home there. Each one of us—tall,
short, fat, thin, cruising through the smooth parts or struggling
through the rough—has all the promise of divinity within her.
When we truly believe that—and that is the essential core of the
gospel message—each one of us, no matter where she starts out
from, can hold up her head, proud and confident. We are truly
the daughters of God, and we have the endless possibilities of
eternity as our heritage.

It's a magnificent prospect, but one of its many advantages
is a very practical, down-to-earth one to help us through our
difficulties now. If we truly appreciate the divine plan for us, we
have the certain knowledge that frees us from the gloom of
guilt and regret, because another central promise of the gospel
is that repentance and Christ's sacrifice make a real difference in
our own particular lives. As ordinary earthly beings, we may do
some consummately dumb things, and we may not often get

close to what we could be, but as long as we're trying our best to be what we know we can be, that is enough. Our potential is important enough that Christ laid down his life for us.

If we look at it that way, maybe we can gather the courage to try to act as if we believe it. But what if even believing all of those things, I still feel that my self-esteem is weak in the knees? All right. Maybe it means taking baby steps at first, clutching on to the promise, and pretending (even to myself) that I feel confident when I don't.

We all have times of feeling that we simply don't know how to go about doing something we've been asked to do. Maybe it's something as basic as walking into the Sunday School class that you've been called to teach (when you don't know anything about teaching, and the prospect of facing those thirteen-year-old show-offs and persuading them to pay attention makes your stomach heave). If you can hang on to the promise— throw your shoulders back and tell yourself firmly that you are a daughter of God and entitled to his help when you are doing his work—you can march straight into that classroom and pretend you are a totally confident adult, and you can be assured that with the Lord's help the playacting can turn into reality. With his help, you can be certain that even those thirteen-year-olds can and will pay attention and learn something during the half hour or so you have together. After all, if the Lord could part the Red Sea and raise Lazarus from the dead, taming a bunch of thirteen-year-olds should be manageable.

Or maybe the problem is at home, where you've made a particularly outrageous misjudgment with your own child. Maybe you were foolishly lax; maybe you were pointlessly severe. Either way, you got shot down in flames, and you find yourself murmuring a hopeless mantra: you're a failure as a mother, you've messed it up again, what are you going to do about it all now, and so forth and so forth. Again, what you need to do is to take a firm grip on your faith, and remember that Jesus laid down his life precisely because we do make those kinds of mistakes and he knew that we would need the promise of repentance to get us past the errors and the sins and the wrong choices.

Leaning on his strength, you can find the confidence and wisdom you need, go find that child, explain where it is you felt you went off the track, and tell him you're sorry and what you intend to do about it. With the sureness of knowing that you have the potential to do it right, this time do what you know you should have done in the first place. The gospel is all about second chances, and we don't need to feel timid about using them.

If we can get the fundamentals right, the trivial stuff—such as walking into parties or knowing what to say in awkward situations or running a meeting when you have to—will take care of itself. Sure, we'll make mistakes along the way. That needn't have anything to do with our self-esteem or our picture of ourselves as daughters of God with eternal potential. After all, the whole plan was based on the certain knowledge that we would make mistakes. It was Satan who had everything organized so we'd all lead flawless lives.

The Father's plan assumed from the beginning that at times we would get things wrong, that we would be lazy and selfish and greedy and irresponsible on occasion, that we would fall flat on our faces from time to time and need to be hauled back up to the upright position and placed on our feet again, and that as long as we kept trying to do the right thing and honestly worked at trying to figure out which were the right choices, mistakes could be erased—through the process of repentance made available by the Atonement—and we could start over in the places that we needed to. Some of us might have easier times than others, but all of us would be placed in a position to learn what we need to know. Each of us has the same potential for eternal growth, and that is solid grounds indeed for self-esteem.

Satan, who would have willed us all to be perfect and who threw away his own chance for progression by insisting on his plan, might whisper in our ears that all is lost and that there's no point in trying further once we've chosen unwisely. But we didn't follow him then and there's no reason to believe him now. Whatever mistakes we may make in the here and now, we have the irrefutable evidence that in that great premortal choice, we chose wisely, because we are here—to learn, to stumble, and with the Lord's help, to pick ourselves up again, knowing that even in the stumbling we have the potential for greatness.

Best of all, if we truly learn to esteem ourselves from that eternal perspective, we can move beyond ourselves and begin to esteem all the others around us—all those other sons and daughters of God who, like us, are trying to learn and develop and who sometimes get it right and sometimes get it spectacularly wrong. We are here to cheer and comfort and irritate each other, and to learn the little lessons and the big ones in company with each other—whether the soul whose path crosses ours is in the guise of an obstreperous young child, or what my daughter calls an old geezer, or even someone as familiar and challenging as a husband. And only when we grow conscious of the value of each of them can we move to the ultimate self-confidence of truly forgetting about ourselves and getting on with the task at hand.

Didn't somebody say something once about whoever loses his life shall find it?

6

On Surviving the Lows

Although all days last twenty-four hours, there are still long days and short days. Wet Wednesdays almost always seem to be the long days that go on longer than it seems reasonable for a day to last. It's the happy, sunny days, the days that you want to savor and stretch, that whip by.

One of the other odd things about having a discouraging day is that, although everybody has them, one of the most characteristic wet Wednesday symptoms is the bleak conviction that you are isolated and alone and that nobody else understands what it is like to feel this way.

One of the first principles to remember, then, about feeling despondent about life in general and your own inadequacies in particular is that feeling that way is not a singular trial that you alone must endure. Everybody else has days of feeling that way, too.

The second principle is that nobody likes it any better than you do.

There are all kinds of discouraging days, of course. There are the typical wet Wednesdays, when you just feel vaguely dissatisfied with yourself and your lot. You know you're going to be happier another day, and, mercifully, you are. Then there are the worse days—fortunately much less frequent—when something has gone seriously wrong. And then there are the worst days of all, generally when you are struggling through some major calamity, when the effort of simply putting one foot ahead of the other demands every resource you can summon up. It's on those days (if you are in a mood to be analytical, which most of us aren't at times like that) that you might be aware of feeling the lick of blackness close enough to begin to understand the depths of the abyss called clinical depression, and to see why those caught up in that excruciatingly painful illness need more help than a hearty thump on the back and loud encouragement to quit glooming and get out and enjoy life.

Even when it's only a once-in-a-while experience associated with some devastating event, to feel that desolate is truly terrible—but unfortunately, it's part of our mortality. Pain was always part of the bargain—unless we remained cradled in the Garden of Eden—and having agreed to try mortality, removed from that pleasant cocoon, we do find ourselves buffeted by adverse circumstances in a challenging world that sometimes doesn't seem to care whether we make it or not. Most unchangeable of all is the searing discovery that if we are going to love people, we are going to know the anguish of losing them. We may know that we will share eternity, but that can feel like little comfort in the cold mornings of waking up to another solitary day. Eternity seems very far away when every fiber of your body is yearning for just a little bit longer of now.

Maybe that's part of the test. The worst part of the discouraging days in general is that on those days it's harder to cling to spiritual certainties. When everything feels as if it's in shambles around you, you can feel estranged from your relationship with the Lord as well. It seems to be an inescapable element for all of us born to this earth: Jesus himself, at the worst moment on the cross, cried out, asking why he was forsaken. So, when we feel most desperately alone, the Lord knows from his own bitter experience exactly what that feels like, and as long as we can hang on to the barest shreds of faith and turn to him, he has promised he will be there. Maybe that's what those bleak days are for—to remind us that we are not expected to meet the challenges and vanquish the demons single-handedly. The only way we can get through the experience of mortality intact is by leaning on the arm of the Lord, and no matter how despondent we may feel, that arm will be there if we can just trust enough to reach out to it.

Not that that means that the troubles shimmer and pop like soap bubbles. The promise is not that nothing will hurt; the promise is that, if we rely on the Lord, we can survive whatever we have to survive. That doesn't mean we're going to like it.

The troubles and trials of ordinary life are sometimes very hard to take. We know that concept in theory—we've been told often that this is a testing time and that much of the reason we're here is to make the right choices when faced with adversity. The trouble is that when we're told that, it is often presented (and heard by us) as if adversity is sort of a bracing tonic, which with the right attitude is really no problem at all—and perhaps, for some, that may be the way it really is.

For most of us, however, adversity is miserable. It's not the same thing for everybody. In my experience, adversity comes in myriad forms. Sometimes it's losing something, or someone, that I wanted very, very badly. Sometimes it's failing, when it mattered that I succeed. Sometimes it's being faced with the intractability of another person's will—maybe one who makes choices I cannot support, no matter how much I love him or her. Sometimes it's being trapped by circumstances I cannot control or see any possible way to escape. Sometimes it seems as if my life has been mysteriously magicked into one of those domino chains of minor or relatively minor mishaps that seem to go on and on, until I begin to wonder fearfully if the chain is infinitely long and if everything that means anything to me is going to go wrong. Sometimes it's a straightforward problem of health, my own or that of someone dear to me, and existence turns into a daily battle of coping with what can be coped with and hunkering down for the rest.

Whatever it is, I don't find that it feels much like a bracing tonic. What it feels like ordinarily varies, depending on the day, from grudgingly tolerable to downright miserable. Knowing that adversity is part of the testing experience—part, in fact, of exactly what we chose to face, back in that time before time, when we chose to come to this earth—doesn't make it any cuddlier.

When you're not facing immediate adversity, I think it's very easy to misinterpret what the gospel teaches us about how to meet hardships, and what strengths are available to us, leaning on the arm of the Lord. Insulated by distance from a problem, it's easy to assume that what's needed is for the person who is facing the problem to develop greater faith and trust in the Lord. Once they do, the reasoning goes, then even if their problem doesn't go away, they will be so sufficiently spiritually uplifted that their distress will conveniently evaporate.

I don't think that's the way it works. I suspect that what most of us pray for most passionately when we are mired in misfortune is for the trouble, whatever it is, to stop. If it takes a miracle to remove the pain, then fine. Let's have the miracle and have it right now. Finding a way to endure what is happening is not ordinarily my first choice as a solution to my difficulties.

And yet it seems to me that that is most often the way the Lord answers our prayers. Oh, of course sometimes a miracle does come along to solve everything, and those miracles are breathtaking and wonderful and faith promoting for everyone around—and they *do* happen. The desperately ill child marvelously rallies and returns uneventfully to health. The wandering husband gets a grip on himself and repents, and the rejuvenated marriage grows closer to what its potential was all along. The financial catastrophe that came frighteningly close abruptly recedes.

But I think that rather more frequently, the way our prayers are answered is by the gift of sufficient strength to hang on regardless. Not that whatever the trial is becomes easy. Not that we become impervious to pain. But somehow, from somewhere, if we rely on the Lord we can find the strength to keep going, one foot in front of the other, even if we hurt. Usually, if we are steadfast, we find the further blessing that eventually, gradually (sometimes it seems by barely perceptible degrees) we can grope out of the shadows and the pain back to something approximating the enjoyment of normal life, and even, in time, unbelievably, to joy. And that, although it may lack the drama of a miracle, is most assuredly our answer to prayer.

I think we sometimes have to remind ourselves of this principle, and we need to be sure to teach it to our children. I don't think we can simply hope that the miracles will come to spare us if we're just worthy enough. I don't really understand the relationship of miracles and worthiness. Sometimes, I suspect, what we need to know we can only learn by trudging through the middle of the swamp of discouragement and difficulty. However worthy we are, we wouldn't be forced into the same growth if we were suddenly rescued by being whipped into a helicopter and flown over the swamp—but even when you recognize that that's true, trudging through a swamp is a lot of work, and while you're doing it you're bound to notice that the helicopter is flying overhead, apparently full of passengers.

That appears to be the way it is and always has been on this earth; for centuries, philosophers have been struggling to produce some thesis to explain why some people seem to be whisked past the physical and spiritual struggles that entangle the rest of us. Maybe they have different kinds of tests than we do, or maybe, for some reason we can't understand now, they don't need to have the tests at all. Whichever way it is really doesn't make much difference to us in the swamp, of course— our job is to keep trudging, without reference to anyone else. We're not being graded on the curve, and how anybody else is doing has nothing to do, really, with what's expected of us. We've been told over and over that the only thing that counts—for us—is how well *we* manage to do what *we* have been given to do. Maybe someday we'll be given the clarity of mind to understand why things happen as they do. Maybe the reasons will all be much more obvious to us when we've gotten past this stage and are looking back at our time here on earth from the clearer perspective of eternity.

Naturally, what makes up our particular swamp is as individual as we are. For some people—those born into abusive, miserable families, for instance—the swamp has the contours of a permanent disaster. I have a friend whose adolescence was a calamity. Her parents' marriage, never a happy one, collapsed; instead of drawing together to give each other strength, the rest of the family, including her mother, retreated into their own misery. The house reeked of unhappiness.

Out of all of them, my friend survived the experience best. At about that time, she was introduced to the Book of Mormon (her family were inactive members of the Church, but her older sister had taken her to Young Women meetings a couple of times), and the words she read spoke straight to her heart. The message she heard was that her Father in Heaven loved her, in spite of what was happening all around her. She was loved. During the lonely evenings, when everybody was locked into their own shells of misery, she would lie on her bed and read her scriptures over and over and over, clinging to that reassurance. Hungry for more of the message, she went to church, to Young Women meetings, to seminary. Eventually, she was old enough to leave home, and she did. She has turned out fine: she is a wife and a mother, and her own home is really a home, with noise and voices and laughter. And the scriptures that she clung to for so long are still an indelible part of her life.

There are few people who can pass through such a calamitous experience unscathed and impervious to the pain. She didn't. In spite of her faithfulness, her family was not miraculously healed. The pain remained. It didn't go away; it didn't get smaller. From experiences outside her family she gained the strength she had to have, and she learned to live with her circumstances (or escape them). Some days were easier than others. Some days, I expect, still are.

A lot more of us are afflicted with more temporary swamps—the kind, perhaps, that dry up in good weather and pose no problems, and then go mushy and marshy with the next hard rain. A lot of us are familiar with the kind of lows that kick in after an accumulation of silly minor stuff that you feel you should be able to shrug off. Maybe you do shrug off these incidents, until your shrugging mechanism overloads and some perfectly trivial setback tips you over the edge. There you are, flailing around with no really sensible reason for feeling bereft and hopeless.

Sometimes the wet Wednesdays suck us under for no better reason than the cyclical nature of a woman's metabolism—although I find there is practically nothing as infuriating as feeling glum or irritable or harassed by some aggravating circumstance (or, worse, accumulation of circumstances) and having someone else tell me, patronizingly, that my only problem is PMS. Even so, and as real as some of the other problems may be, the fact is that we live in our bodies, and a lot of us grow familiar with the roller-coaster ride of a typical month.

For a lot of women, the ups and downs are insignificant, more a matter of convenience or inconvenience than anything else. But for some of us the highs are higher than the average and the lows are lower—and perversely, even knowing that this is one of the days when I'm likely to feel that the world's after me doesn't mean that I *don't* feel that the world's after me. Knowing I'm irritable, I still get much crabbier than I would usually be over such admittedly trivial irritations as children's shoes abandoned in the middle of the front hall or the exasperating inability of the washing machine repairman to show up when I was promised he would. Being prepared for feeling sulky doesn't mean I don't feel sulky.

However it affects us, the fact is that women's bodies are geared for an amazing variety of extremely complex functions. It really ought not to be that surprising that sometimes all the unconscious machinery at work produces effects that intrude into our conscious awareness. After all, men's bodies are complicated enough, and all they do is sustain their own lives. We do all that and are capable of nurturing and maintaining separate life within us as well. No wonder we are awash in a fluctuating hormonal cocktail in which sometimes the ingredients are in a comfortable balance and sometimes they aren't. But whether they are or not, we have to keep going through the day, job after job after job, and there are days—the wet Wednesdays—when that's hard.

There are other discouraging days, though, when the gloomy feeling is more amorphous, and there doesn't seem to be any logical explanation for it. Sometimes, I suspect, we just get weary of the struggle to be good, of trying to make the right choices all the time and be the best our potential allows. It doesn't help that Satan is at our shoulder, whispering in our ear that what's asked of us is really unreasonably hard, that nobody should be expected to keep impossible standards, and that even aiming for perfection is a quixotic, lunatic quest that will inevitably end in frustration. As usual, his argument is appealing enough to make his twisted, inaccurate portrayal of the situation sound plausible.

Christ's message to us was not only that we should be doing the right things but that we should be doing them for the right reasons, and that is, in truth, an enormous assignment. He is preparing us for perfection. We won't get there today, and we won't get there tomorrow, but we have the possibilities for perfection within us, and today we can be closer than we were yesterday, and tomorrow, closer than we are today.

Unfortunately, that's not an idea that our larger society is very enthusiastic about right now. There is a lot of interest in self-help and self-improvement, but the emphasis is on the *self.* There doesn't seem to be much interest in the idea of standards that have independent reality: what's right or wrong to do is discussed in terms of what works, or what people think is important, or what is most convenient for the greatest number of people. The idea that a given action is wrong, or sinful, no matter what the consensus of the moment might be, is one that seems to make a lot of people uncomfortable.

Maybe the problem started when people overenthusiastically applied the principle of democracy. It's one thing to maintain that the laws of the land should be decided by the representatives chosen by the majority of the voters. The here-and-now laws, after all, only have reality when we decide what they are. But there are also the eternal laws, which shape ultimate reality. Those laws are fixed laws, immutable and unchanging. They would be the same even if only one out of a hundred—or a thousand, or a billion—believed they were true.

Take the basic fundamental law that sexual experience is to be restricted to the precincts of marriage, for example. That's pretty fundamental, and for the last few centuries this law was pretty much taken as a given within Christian society. Of course, that doesn't mean that everybody obeyed the law—free agency is free agency, after all, and that particular law exists to govern a very powerful impulse. There have always been those who chose not to be so governed.

But there was general agreement that the law was there, that it existed. When it was disobeyed, people recognized that they had been disobedient. The resulting social pressure didn't make the law any more or less true, of course, but it did help to define the boundaries of behavior, and it provided a useful bulwark against temptation for a lot of people. One of the things that is most dangerous about our society now is that those certainties no longer exist. Our own convictions aren't necessarily bolstered comfortably by the agreement of our larger society. The struggles that good, honest folk have always had with

temptation—some of which are mirrored in our greatest literature—are now interpreted as period pieces, out-of-date, and
even kind of pathetic.

The general consensus now appears to be that extramarital
sex is no longer necessarily wrong, exactly. Unwise, perhaps. A
decision not to be taken lightly, yes. But wrong? Well—as all
too many of our columnists and talk show hosts and other
shapers of public morality would say—you have to look at the
individual circumstances.

As Latter-day Saints, we simply don't believe that. The individual circumstances are irrelevant. "Thou shalt not" was the
commandment that Moses brought down, and that's the commandment that has been reiterated over and over again since. It
hasn't changed. *We* might have changed in a lot of external,
superficial ways since the time of Moses, but none of those
changes mean that we don't have to obey the same laws he presented or face the consequences of breaking those laws. (It
might be pointed out that our society as a whole is currently
facing the consequences of society-wide promiscuity, with the
epidemic of incurable sexually transmitted disease being at least
in part attributable to such promiscuity. The law is the law. The
Lord has not always given us a full explanation of all the reasons
for the laws—and indeed we should not require such an explanation before we are willing to obey—but given the risk of con-
tracting a disease such as AIDS, the wisdom of observing the
law of chastity is all the more obvious.)

Worldly influences don't make the hard parts of trying to
bring our lives into line with the eternal principles any easier,
and sometimes, the empty, bleak feeling of the bad days may
simply originate in the uncomfortable knowledge that we're
falling short somewhere along the line.

Guilt is another fact unpopular according to today's no-
tions, but that unpopularity doesn't mean it doesn't exist. It
still does the job it's there to do: it serves as a nagging reminder
that something is not as it should be. Obviously all the bad days
don't come along because we're doing something we shouldn't,
or not doing something we should, but probably more of them
do than we're inclined to admit. The world doesn't help any by
trying to comfort us with the fallacy that it's not important
anyway.

It's hard enough to do daily battle over our natural impulses to do the easy, less righteous things (go ahead, lose your temper—at least for the moment it feels good to just snap out what you're thinking, and if your speaking your mind means being unkind to somebody else, that's their look-out, not yours). It's harder when the climate of opinion around you seems to imply that whether or not you lose your temper doesn't matter, really, and that self-control and kindness to others are fine, but the important thing is not to bottle up your own frustrations.

So say I do lose my temper. In the aftermath, I may no longer be frustrated, but I probably also have a deal of fence-mending to do with the unfortunate people who happened to be in the line of fire. Even more important, I have a quiet, shamed feeling deep inside myself; I know perfectly well that I let down my own standards, many of which are eternal as well as personal. Now I have to cope with the consequences, not the least of which is that it's hard to find much comfort in prayer when you have just finished telling somebody off noisily and hurtfully. Even assuming that the somebody is sufficiently Christian to forgive me immediately, it's hard to forgive myself.

In a way, our weariness and sadness when we know full well that we've disregarded a major or minor commandment (whether or not the world around us recognizes that as a problem) are positive evidences of our potential freedom from earth stains. We've been promised joy, but the joy only comes when we can leave our mortal imperfections behind.

The full job won't be done this side of Resurrection Day, but we can have tastes of it here and there. There is the wonderful floating relief of finally carrying out an obligation that we've too long postponed. Maybe it's finally making an apology that for ages we knew needed making, but we kept waiting for the easy opportunity, which never presented itself. Maybe it's getting tithing or fast offerings up to date, when I've been putting it off from week to week, telling myself that I keep forgetting to pick up an envelope but half knowing that I've been using the money set aside as a comfortable cushion to absorb any inaccuracies in my check-balancing efforts. Maybe it's any one of a hundred similar efforts, small in themselves but astoundingly liberating in effect once made.

Sins and faults negate the possibility of serenity. Envy and jealousy, unkindness, dishonesty, swiftness to judge—all the stupid little moral failures, and even more so the big ones—are not wrong only because the Lord said they were; they're wrong because they lead inevitably to misery and guilt and bitterness.

There's envy, for example. In the Ten Commandments we were told we should not be covetous. That may not be the word most of us would use now, but we still know what it means and we can still find ourselves caught up in it. Whether you call it covetousness or envy or keeping up with the Joneses, given its head, it can eat away at you.

In the tenth commandment the focuses of covetousness are detailed as houses and manservants and maidservants and oxen and asses (not to mention the neighbor's wife). Few of us spend a lot of time sighing enviously over the neighbor's oxen these days (although perhaps an equivalent to coveting the maidservant would be glooming because there's a cleaning-service car in the neighbor's driveway, and I'm on my hands and knees doing my own kitchen floor), but the emotion is alive and well. We can be envious of new dining room furniture, or a trip to the Caribbean, or children who appear to be spontaneously well behaved, or a comfortable income that eliminates financial anxiety, or social success, or a pretty face or shapely body.

Whatever it may be, envy doesn't help. It doesn't cheer you up or make doing without any of those things any easier. It's just depressing. In fact, envy is a horrible feeling. It destroys your own pleasure in whatever you do have, or can do, or see in your own mirror, and it inevitably distorts your relationship with the person you are envying—and none of this, needless to say, enhances the rest of what's going on in your life, either.

But envy isn't the only thing, of course, that will account for an uncomfortable awareness that I am not only out of sorts but out of tune with the Spirit as well. Knowing I have been deliberately unkind will do it. Few of us, of course, set out to be deliberately unkind, but it's surprising how easily it happens when someone unwittingly (or even wittingly) provokes us to the point that we lash out with words that hurt, and are meant to. It happens particularly easily, unfortunately, with those closest and dearest to us.

The intimacy of marriage means that husbands and wives

know enough about each other to know exactly what words will stop the other dead in his or her tracks. This terrible ability to hurt each other is the sinister other face of our ability to comfort each other—and a lot of the bitterness of divorce rises out of the fact that that weapon of knowledge is the one that was ultimately wielded.

Even short of that, wives can and do say things that can only be described as deliberately unkind, and so do their husbands. The problem for our peace of mind is that after the heat of battle cools and the warmth of reconciliation takes over, it's unhappily easy to remember just what you said—even if it makes you feel wormish, now that you're not so angry—and equally hard to wholly believe your own rationalizations about why you said it.

Losing control of our tongues is another way in which we estrange ourselves from our original intention of working toward perfection (for why else did we come to this earth anyway?). And when this happens we are, unsurprisingly, gloomy and depressed, and we feel empty and unsatisfied. Do you suppose part of the trouble could be the vaguest whiff of memory of what we set out to do?

The big sins are obvious obstacles—and adultery, no matter how ingeniously and painstakingly we rationalize it, is still adultery—but we need to be aware of the other, less dramatic ones, too: envy and unkindness, of course, and being judgmental, and being dishonest. Living what are undoubtedly good lives overall, we get tangled up in expediency and taking shortcuts with the truth, and we find ourselves troubled and unhappy, and unable to pinpoint just what exactly the problem is. It's all very discouraging—or it would be, without the saving grace of repentance and the chance to shut the door firmly on yesterday's stupidities and start over.

For what it's worth, we are not the first to feel hopeless, from time to time, about the intractability of our weaknesses and the frequency of our wrong choices. The medieval scholars and theologians had a name for it. They called it *despair,* and listed it as one of the seven deadly sins, right up there with lust and avarice and pride. Despair, they said, was a deadly sin because it had elements of blasphemy: despair denied that the power of God was great enough to bring you back into the light.

Those scholars and theologians, stumbling around in the darkness of apostasy, got a lot of things wrong, but I'm inclined to think they had that one about right. The Light of Christ is always there, whether or not we can see it. We can feel it there on the sunny days, when we move in unconscious harmony with the laws and teachings of the prophets and consequently our whole lives flow with a smooth rhythm (when the baby cries you mind it less because she's so soft against your cheek, and you remember all the delicious reasons you love your husband), but it is just as much there on the wet Wednesdays, when we feel estranged and distant. Whether we can see it plainly or not, the Light of Christ is there. We were never meant to succeed without his help, any more than the gasoline engine was meant to roar on without fuel. We are designed to function at our best only when we are relying on the Lord and his light.

Some days we may have to repeat that to ourselves over and over—the way we teach our children to say "please" and "thank you"—but as long as we can hang on to that principle, by sheer determination of will if no other way, we can work our way back out to that light. We may not find it today. Maybe not tomorrow. But as long as we hang in there and endure, the Lord's hand will be there to uplift us, whether we are in a state of mind to recognize it or not. Sometimes it's only afterwards, looking back, that we see it all as it truly was and are genuinely amazed that we didn't identify the source of our strength at the time.

And sometimes we remember that we learned that on the next wet Wednesday that comes along, and sometimes we don't.

7

On
Measuring Up

So what is good enough anyway? We know what it feels like to fall short—of our own expectations, if not of anybody else's. But how do we know if things are getting any better or (heaven forbid) worse? How do we keep track? In school we got report cards. Sometimes they were right on track and sometimes you wondered if you and the teacher had inhabited the same classroom, but either way, you got them. If you went on to work, there were performance reports, formal or informal: someone else was keeping an eye on how you were doing, however the feedback was delivered to you. But for our most important job, the job of being a person, being a wife, being a mother—what kind of feedback do we get on that?

The difficulty is certainly not that there isn't any feedback. There's lots. As long as we live with other people it pours back at us: "I know you're tired, but you're awfully grouchy." "That back hall closet is getting to be a mess again—I can't find a thing in there." "Honey, you look great tonight." "Everybody else's mother lets them watch *Saturday Night Live*—what do you think I am, a baby or something?" "Why didn't you get my green top washed? I put it in the laundry." "You're the most wonderful mother in the world." "After all these years, you would think that you would have figured out that I hate those scratchy socks." "Wow, it looks nice in here—are we having company?" "You never listen to a word I say." "I do love you." "I wish we could have a sensible adult discussion without you getting that edge in your voice." "The kitchen floor is sticky, Mom." "I'm not snapping at you, you're snapping at me." "G'night, Mommy. I love you." "I go out with a perfectly nice boy and it's like the Spanish Inquisition when I come home— where did you go, what did you see—don't you understand anything about privacy?" "You never let *us* have a hamster when we were in second grade. You're spoiling him." "Oh, thanks, Mom. I knew you'd remember." "What did you do to your hair? I liked it the old way." "So I told him my mom had already explained about that, and he said . . . " "Mom, she's been in my sweater drawer again. Why do you let her?"

Oh, the feedback rains around us. In my own personal experience there is, however, one small problem with it: it usually has a lot more to do with what's going on in the head of the person delivering it than it does with a dispassionate review of my performance. There is also the point that there's seldom partial credit for effort. Either I succeeded at whatever was on the top of the list of the evaluator (in which case I am Queen for a Day or, more likely, taken for granted, like the wallpaper), or I managed to forget or botch up or overrule whatever it was (in which case I am the blight of the household). It doesn't seem to matter that I was trying.

If our children have their own agendas uppermost in their minds, so, usually, do our husbands. In fairness, however, do we give them a carefully thought out analysis of their performance either? What we probably do is just about what they do: remark admiringly about the good things we notice, and crab about the irritating things (or decide nobly not to crab, and grumble to ourselves about them instead), and do either one spontaneously as the occasion arises.

Which is about what we also do with parents or close friends, if those are the ones nearest and dearest to us. There is a difference, however. We often choose to subtract something from a parent's approving remarks on the grounds that they are dotingly prejudiced, or from their criticisms on the grounds that it's more of the same old thing we've been hearing for years. There is also the point that friends, unless they are extra-ordinarily intimate and of long standing, don't know enough about the overall pattern of our lives to do more than make passing comments—some of which, true enough, can be amaz-ingly illuminating. Sometimes it takes an outsider, in a casual aside, to draw your attention to something in your ordinary, everyday life that you simply hadn't focused on before, and there is a sudden, eye-opening "So maybe that is what's hap-pening here!"

Still, there's nothing wrong with feeling wistful about the fact that outside assessments of our efforts tend to be so erratic. The impulse to seek some kind of evaluation is a perfectly human one. We all want to know how we're doing from time to time—even in games, we keep score.

If we're going out to work, somebody keeps track of how we're doing, and usually we hear about it one way or another. We may not always like what we're told, but the feedback is there, and we can use it to adjust our future course. One of the main frustrations of being a stay-at-home mom is that most evaluation (as opposed to the hit-and-miss comments made in passing) is self-evaluation. If everything goes smoothly every-body assumes it happened by itself, and you can go for days without anybody noticing that you've done anything—unless you rearrange the living room furniture single-handedly while everybody else is out, so that when they come back there's a chair where the path to the dining area used to be. There is also the unfortunate fact that the most obvious way to try to check on how we're getting along is to compare ourselves with the other moms we encounter, which way lies frustration unless we can ruthlessly tear competition from our hearts. In any case, the competition is meaningless: even if our houses happened to be absolutely identical, the families living inside them would never be.

Valid outside evaluation for a stay-at-home mom may be rare. Valid outside evaluation of *anybody's* spiritual accomplish-ments is probably impossible—unless the Lord is the evaluator. Only you and he know what goes on in the quiet of your soul.

It's easy to forget about that quiet inner center of our being, our truest self. The outside world is so noisy! Of course, most of the outside world has chosen to forget about the existence of a soul, much less the possibility of the inner peace that comes with obedience, and yet that peace is what we seem to have a universal hunger for. When that's in place, we can sustain remarkable buffetings of circumstance. Without it, we are quite literally hollow at the core.

Nobody else knows much about what's going on in my soul. Oh, home teachers and visiting teachers may ask how I'm doing, and there are the periodic interviews with the bishop and the stake president, but all they can do is take soundings—listen to the echoes, so to speak. The real function of those interviews, after all, is to serve as a catalyst in helping me think about my own spiritual state. Maybe an interview comes along when my life is flowing easily, and I look deep inside to find tranquility and light and certainty. Rather more often, I'm afraid, I peer sheepishly into a garden that needs weeding—the general shape is just fine, but it has a neglected, forgotten look where spiritual requirements have been pushed aside to make room for daily routine. That shouldn't happen, but it does. So how do we evaluate that?

How *are* we coming? How good do we need to be? Christ challenged us with perfection, and against perfection, anything else looks shabby. That's simply a fact, and we have to work out our own individual ways to cope with the situation. The method advocated by many in the world (urged on by the whisperings of Satan) is to insist that perfection is impossible, so we might as well come to terms with where we are now, and develop our self-esteem based on that, however unsatisfactory some aspects of our spiritual and temporal development might be if measured against any external standards.

As sisters in the gospel, we have to take the point of view that even though perfection in the here and now may be unlikely, our most important assignment is to stretch and grow as much as our spirits are capable of, and perfection is what we aim for, even if we can predict in advance that we'll fall short.

Yes, falling short can be discouraging, but not trying at all is literally soul destroying. Besides, when we're in a good spell, we can usually handle a certain amount of routine failure. We try it again, get absorbed in what we're doing, and the days roll past. There isn't always the need for introspection.

The problems come up on the wet Wednesdays, when for

one reason or another we seem to bump to a halt. Typically, I find myself looking around at all the ordinary things I'm doing—running endless errands; washing faces and floors; keeping control of my tongue and temper when presented with more than sufficient provocation to let fly; shuttling back and forth from the church, with manuals and scriptures and dishes and stuff to take there and stuff to take home—and wonder what the point of it all is. Sometimes I suspect that somehow I got conned into this swirl of miscellaneous responsibilities, and when I'm particularly discouraged, I wonder how long it will be before I feel I'm achieving anything, and sometimes it's very hard to see any perceptible progress. Perfection feels infinitely far away, and everyday chores seem a most unlikely method of ever attaining it, anyhow. That's when I feel the sharpest need for some way of measuring, some way of determining if I'm moving forward or drifting in unproductive circles. At those times I need some way of measuring my achievements, such as they are.

On those dreary wet Wednesdays, to believe in the possibility of making any significant achievements may require a leap of faith, but it's a leap of faith we must take. Sometimes we really need to work all the way back to the basics to figure out where we stand.

In some ways the gospel is like the humble onion, made up of layer upon layer, right down to the core. Yes, starting from the outside, we believe in the Word of Wisdom and tithing and genealogy; and yes, moving another layer within, we believe in the restored gospel and that Joseph Smith was a prophet, seer, and revelator in these latter days; and yes, another layer down, we believe that Jesus Christ was physically born on this earth and physically died, and in doing so took on the burden of our sins so that the doors of repentance could swing open to give us the opportunity for eternal life; and yes, when we stand at the center, we believe that the only reason that we were worth such a magnificent sacrifice is that we are in the most literal sense the spirit daughters and sons of our Heavenly Father and that each one of us carries an elemental spark of divinity within us. If we are truly to have faith in God and in the gospel, then we have to have faith in ourselves and our own potential, because that is what lies at the very heart of our beliefs.

The other fundamental truth is just as simple. The only key that will unlock our great potential is our trust in Jesus Christ and our obedience to his principles. Achieving virtue—indeed, achieving anything but the most superficial forms of competence—is impossible without the Lord. The harder we try to make it on our own, the more certainly we fail.

This is not a concept new to us in our time. We have at least two well-documented demonstrations of the phenomenon: the Old Testament and the Book of Mormon. In both historical accounts, the chosen people start out relying on the Lord and his strength, and everything goes well. Everything goes so well, in fact, that the people come to the conclusion that they're managing splendidly on their own. Having decided that they can clearly handle their lives themselves, they drift away from obedience—which inevitably leads to a consequent drift from virtue—and fall straight off the precipice into failure and disaster. Disaster multiplies on disaster until, humbled, the chosen people turn back to the Lord and reorganize their lives around obedience again, and the cycle begins all over. The scenario never changes, only the personnel.

Now it's our turn, and the rules are still the same.

That's not the way the world sees it, of course. In the eyes of the world, the scriptures are interesting and have comforting patches—and, of course, there are passages that do have to be considered as great literature—but in practical terms, says the world, they don't have much to do with life now. After all, the melancholy chronicles of the tribulations of ancient groups of pastoral people don't have much to do with our problems in the post-industrial world, do they?

It's not very fashionable these days to believe in our God-given potential and in the inevitable results of disobedience and a devaluing of virtue, whether or not they're demonstrated in the scriptures. By and large, the world chooses to see itself as populated by ordinary people, capable at times of noble behavior, perhaps, but generally trudging along motivated by decent self-interest. We get along, and that's about as much as we should expect.

The world expects so little of us because the world believes we are ordinary and fallible. As believers in the gospel, we have to expect a lot more of ourselves, because we know that though fallible we may be, we have (as we have always had) the potential for perfection—maybe not here, and maybe not now, but as long as we are working in that direction and have our hand in the hand of the Lord, we have space much wider than here and time much longer than now. Perfection *is* possible. Falling short is one circumstance of mortality. Picking ourselves up, dusting off, and getting back at it is another.

There are lots of ways to regroup and start over, which is hardly surprising when you remember that it's something everybody has to do—as unlikely as that may seem when you look around, and in your world of ordinary weekdays or Sundays everybody else seems to be on top of things, polished, content, handbag organized, and shepherding docile daughters with hair not only combed and curled but fitted out with ribbons that match. Exactly where those paragons might come up short is their problem, and really none of our business, but the fact is that they certainly do, and given the amazing range of human individuality, it is not surprising that there are different ways of picking yourself up and getting going again.

Figuring out which way is the best way for you as an individual to haul yourself back to your feet and plan a program for progress is a matter of equal parts of prayer and determination. Neither part works on its own; it takes the combination.

One old standard method for organizing progress is goal setting, and the main reason it is an old standard is that it works for a lot of people a lot of the time, and it's not hard to see why it works. The business of setting goals helps us focus on improvement.

For one thing, setting goals is not the kind of thing anybody can do while daydreaming about something else. If you are going to be serious about it, it requires that you sit down and think about what you've been doing and what you want to do differently. What you want to work on can be something as eminently practical as getting a handle on the backyard garden that has been used to grow some cabbage (of which the worms took more than their share), lettuce, tomatoes, and unbelievable quantities of zucchini, which doesn't happen to be your family's favorite. Write that down as a goal, then. Producing a well-organized, productive garden is not precisely brain surgery: what mainly needs to take place is sensible planning, careful preparation of the soil, and persistent, season-long willingness to get out there and do what has to be done, because your attention may wander, but that of the weeds and garden pests will not.

Besides, it's invigorating being out in the fresh air, and newly turned earth is very satisfactory. There are even those who claim that it is fragrant, but most of the people who love to sit back on their heels and savor the aroma of the dirt they're working don't need to set goals to get their gardens under control, because gardening is their recreation, and they'll do it no matter what else is going on, the same way you make pottery or read books or do cross-stitch or whatever happens to be your thing. The gardeners can put these other activities down as *their* goals.

Or maybe your goal is a spiritual one—maybe to pick up the Book of Mormon or the Bible or one of the other books of scripture and read it, not chapter by chapter, but thought by thought; and instead of sliding over the sections where in all honesty you can't figure out what they're talking about, you stop and study it out and maybe look through some scriptural commentaries and pray until you get enough of a glimmering so that you can let it go and move forward. In other words, really read. That's a worthy goal.

Or, there is the old perennial about losing that twenty pounds. Well, so what? That may not be the most spiritual effort you ever made, but it is perfectly true that one of the reasons we came to this earth was to learn to control our appetites, and while our appetite for food may not be the most threatening to our soul's peace, nonetheless, as we who've tried it know, disciplining your mind and body to consume less food than you want requires constant vigilance and determination. Unfortunately, that's the only way to do it. The soaring national debt and the creeping credit card balance (where we spent today's money yesterday) require that we pay for past indulgence with present self-denial—and the same can often be said of that extra twenty pounds. In a sense, you ate for today last week and last month, and maybe even last year sometime. Unfortunately, neither the taste nor the memory are likely to linger on long enough to enliven the distressingly low-calorie, high-fiber, low-fat munchies which are all you can allow yourself now. Also, it doesn't take long to discover that an essential secondary element of the self-discipline of dieting involves self-discipline in talking about it, because no matter how much the subject of dieting may be on the mind of the dieter, most nondieters in the immediate area are not enthralled by a blow-by-blow account of your fixation on what does or doesn't go into your mouth.

Goal setting does work. You identify what you want to work on, work out what the intermediate steps are between where you are now and where you want to get, and then actually take the steps and get the enormous satisfaction of climbing up the ladder. There you are, measuring visible, honest-to-goodness progress. You can get there. It works—it really, truly works.

In fact, the reality that it works so well can turn into a pitfall for those of us who tend to be enthusiasts and figure that if a little bit is good, a whole lot is better. Having discovered that setting one goal is so wonderfully successful (in my case too often even before I've actually achieved the initial goal), I rush out and set a whole bunch more, and I think that I see earthly perfection finally within my grasp.

What happens, of course, is perfectly predictable. What makes goal setting work is concentration and persistence—keeping one goal firmly in mind and proceeding steadfastly towards it. As soon as I have goals on all sides, it's a scattershot situation. Nobody can dash off in a dozen different directions at once, and what I end up with is long lists of things I'm not doing and the frustrated sense of not having measured up—again.

To be honest, of course, it isn't always misplaced enthusiasm that gets me into that bind. There are spells when it seems that every Church class I attend or auxiliary I serve in is presenting goals for me to adopt as my own. Sometimes that goal may dovetail nicely with a private goal I want to work on as well; sometimes, I guess, I just have to reinterpret the teacher's earnest "Let's all make this our goal" into "I think this is important and would like you to think about it, too"—which isn't exactly the same thing at all. After all, goals are meant to help and encourage. When they just turn into another burden—when just plain setting goals has become the goal—it's time to turn away and try to think of another way to move ahead.

Sometimes instead of setting more goals to achieve more things, what we need to do is to delete some. (Or, if you're a truly dedicated goal setter, think of it as setting a goal of reorganizing priorities.) The feeling of being pressured is hardly an unfamiliar one to women who are active in the Church and who have family lives, for the most obvious of reasons—we're often trying to do more than twenty-four hours will accommodate. Being busy and productive is a happy feeling; being pressured is not.

What tips one individual woman over from one to the other is a wholly individual matter. We were not all endowed with the same energy level, and we are trying to meet different demands. Some of us married men who seem to need more from their wives than our friends' husbands do. It's not necessarily that anything's wrong with that sort of man, or with us; it's simply that the pattern of our marriages requires more concentration from us than other wives might have to give on an ordinary basis, although all marriages go through patches when they need extra effort. Our children, too, as we swiftly discover, run from the top to the bottom of the range in the amount of time and attention they need from their mothers.

Some of us are trying to keep a job going outside of the home, and some of us are having a struggle to keep home going at home. Whatever it might be that contributes to the cumulative total, there is no mistaking the overwhelmed feeling of falling hopelessly behind all over the place.

The easy counsel is to cut back on something. The hard part is deciding what. Few of us spend substantial time lolling on the furniture and popping chocolate bonbons in our mouths, which is a pity, as that would be such a natural candidate for deletion. Our choices are usually a lot harder.

One way to start deciding what to eliminate is to make a stringently accurate record of what you're trying to do now. This is most directly accomplished by simply writing down what you do all day long for a day or two, or for as long as you can stand it. Let's be honest: this is a major bore to do, since if you're going to record each change in occupation, you inevitably spend an uncommon amount of time solemnly checking the clock and writing things down. (In fact, you should probably give yourself a half hour's credit at the end of the day for record keeping.) Ideally, this will give you some idea of where your time is vanishing, and what it is you actually do that may be different from what you think you do. When you have identified what it is that takes up your time, you can look at it all and ask a couple of hard questions: what can be done only by me, and what can I get somebody else to do if I invest the necessary teaching time and follow-up supervision?

You may have to be ruthless about it, but when you really look at what all of your responsibilities are, they do divide up surprisingly easily into the two categories. Some things, such as nursing babies and fixing weekend breakfasts with the whole family in the kitchen and after-dinner chats with your husband, demand not only your time but also your attention—and it has to be *you* who does them. If you're unavoidably unavailable, they either don't happen or some entirely different substitute has to be worked out.

Some things, such as doing laundry and changing sheets and vacuuming the living room and doing the grocery shopping, could be done by anybody, but you're the one who usually does them, because you know how. That doesn't mean you have to. Although it certainly seems initially that it's easier just to get in and get the job done rather than get into the whole educational process of training a recruit to do it, that's only considering the short term. Long term, they need to learn and you need the help—even if you do have to spend some time locating your recruits, who tend to disappear casually when they sense that the cleaning tools are being assembled. After all, your painfully acquired timetable of actual activities has spoken: look at those jobs carefully. Right there is your slack.

One thing that isn't slack are the miscellaneous minutes you grab for yourself or that dribble away in little bits here and there—unless, of course, they threaten to multiply and overwhelm the pattern of your day. But three minutes here, spent staring out the kitchen window as you halfway contemplate the roses on the point of bloom and halfway decide whether to start upstairs in the bedrooms or downstairs with the wash, or the extra five minutes there, in the shower as you savor the relaxing warmth of hot water on your back, are not slack. It is perfectly true that there are efficiency experts who would insist that those wasted minutes can be turned into productive hours, but don't let them get to you—even computers take downtime. So should we.

Nor, when we're trying to cut back on our activities, should we necessarily attempt to rearrange our responsibilities so that nobody but us encounters any disruption. If your choices of what to eliminate lie between things that are important to the children, things that are important to your husband, and things that are important to you, you can't always decide that it is only your things that have to be discarded.

There are a couple of extremely practical reasons why that doesn't work. In the first place, whether they consciously recognize it or not, the ordinary daily requirement that is the most important to both the children and your husband is your own continued mental health. If part of reducing your stress level means that your son will not have his mother at the sidelines of every single game (but she still squeezes out time to work occasionally on her picture framing), better that he adjust to that than that he try to cope with a mother who swings between tight-lipped irritability and bursting into tears over minor setbacks because she's been going too far too hard for too long and hasn't touched any of her own personal projects for weeks.

The same principle holds true for husbands. You can do business entertaining and help with his hobbies and run the errands so he can work uninterrupted until you turn blue, but your marriage is unlikely to flourish when most of the time you're emotionally inaccessible—or physically present but absentminded and unresponsive—either because you're locked into the entertaining, errand running, and so on or because you're plain worn out.

The other problem is that very few of us can consistently plow our own interests under in the service of others (even greatly loved others) without feeling a bit like a noble martyr, and noble martyrs are not the most comfortable house companions. Ideally, of course, we become capable of unlimited unselfishness. Maybe that's where we get to in the next stage. Maybe there are even some of us who are there now, but most of us find we can manage short spurts of wholehearted unselfishness, but short spurts are about it. Nor do most of us live with families sufficiently observant and unselfish, themselves, to notice continuous sacrifice and restore us with gratitude and consideration. What generally seems to happen is that every-body around you takes your self-denial for granted and pro-ceeds to expect more of it, and you wind up as an extremely well-developed doormat, albeit a puzzled, aggrieved one. It is not that hard to figure out when that is happening. The glory of God *is* intelligence, and it can be applied to solving the most unexciting, everyday problems.

I find that pruning back on the self-expectations is one way to cope when the growth of goals—which were, after all, origi-nally to help me keep track of my progress—has gotten out of control. Another way is simply to shelve some of them for the time being. That way I can comfort myself with the promise that I still have every intention of developing my genealogical skills and getting involved in community services and clearing out the basement and learning to think before I speak and doing everything else that's on my giant list, but this week and maybe next I'll just concentrate on being calm and consistent in my treatment of squabbling offspring and getting (and keep-ing) up to date with the ironing and mending.

We've all heard the talks or read the articles that discuss the what-if-your-life-ended-today question—well, take a break and hope it won't and work on the couple of things that are making you feel most defeated. There is, after all, a decent probability that we'll still be around next week, or the week after, and maybe then we'll feel heartened enough by our limited suc-cesses to find new energy to undertake more of the items on our lists.

Or at least that's the way it should work. Sometimes no readjustment seems to work, and we just grind to a halt. It all seems pointless, as if all we're doing is making lists of things we aren't doing, and what we thought were manageable goals seem to recede tantalizingly, forever just beyond our reach. It is all very frustrating.

At those times, it may help to take a complete break, and instead of looking forward to figure out where you are and where you're going, take a look backward to where you were and see how far you've managed to come. Reminding yourself of what you have actually improved on can be very comforting sometimes, and remembering that there are battles that you're no longer fighting can encourage you to press forward on the ones in which you haven't yet succeeded. Keeping your temper may not yet be an accomplished fact, maybe, but you are reading the scriptures regularly, and it's been months since you forgot an orthodontist appointment. Those may not be major accomplishments to anyone else (except maybe the exasperated orthodontist), but of such minutiae is the ladder to perfection constructed. You are entitled to pat yourself—gently—on the back. You may not be near perfection yet, but you're doing better than you were before.

One thing that we really can't do when we measure our progress (hard to resist as it may be) is to take credit, or blame, for what other people do or fail to do—even those as near to us as our children and husbands.

That's not the way it feels, of course. When your son finally rewards you, with a magnificent public performance, for all the money spent on piano lessons and all the hours it's taken driving him back and forth and supervising practice time, you glow with pride—pride for him, of course, but also pride for you. Or, when your daughter, having been more or less strong-armed into participation in the speech festival, bails out at the last moment and informs the director that she isn't taking part after all, you feel not only as if *she's* let everyone down but as if *you* have as well. But whatever it feels like, it was his success and it was her choice not to compete. Certainly you had an advisory role, but that's what it was, advisory. The sensible advisor knows that credit or blame are the province of the person who accepted or rejected the advice.

The fact to which we have to adjust, in our emotions as much as in our heads, is that those dear people, as precious to us as they are, are still themselves, endowed with their own particular capacity to triumph and to make mistakes, and their own free agency to choose which it will be. The eternal principle of free agency means that they must necessarily carry the responsibility for themselves. Obviously we all have influence on each other, but just as you must ultimately decide what you are going to do about all those influences (from the ads on television on up) that are trying to sway you, so your children and even your husband must decide for themselves what to do about you and your influence on them.

This isn't something we think about a lot with the children when they are small, of course—it's our job then to teach and guide, and their job to learn, and one of the engaging things about little children is that, by and large, they aren't fighting it. They may have strong feelings (when they're around age two) about who puts on shoes and socks, or when to get off the swing, but in general they're pretty amenable. They like to learn, and follow you around obligingly, and they beam all over when they've pleased you.

This changes.

When they're young, you worry that you might be making mistakes; as they get older, they point your mistakes out to you. Little by little they grow into their free agency, and with the determination, which all growing human beings have, to take command of their own destiny, they'll jerk the control out of your hands if you're not quick enough to pass it over—and few of us are, about everything. Sometimes we loosen the reins too much and sometimes we hold them too tight: shepherding a child into adulthood is about the most complicated job any of us will ever undertake, and we're bound to get it wrong sometimes. Are we doing enough? Are we saying the right things at the right time? Are we teaching with wisdom and gentleness? Does the example they see us set match up with the principles we're trying to explain to them?

Probably not, at least not all of the time. All of us have been reared by imperfect parents, and it seems unlikely that our children are sufficiently blessed to be endowed with the first generation of parental perfection. Like our own parents, we get tired and grumpy, and we have our own failings and idiosyncrasies to battle. We jump to conclusions and speak when it would have been better to listen—or are silent when our children need to have our counsel.

Many of our mistakes are born out of love. We know from experience where the potholes are, and we try to guide our children safely past—and sometimes the guidance is with an all-too-firm hand. We know that if we could just control the situation we could keep them safe—and yet control was Satan's plan, and as we recognize the pitfalls of that plan, so we can appreciate with greater gratitude the plan that was chosen. The longing for control over the choices of the people we love is an insidious temptation: it's a good thing that the possibility of possessing that control does not exist.

With rueful gratitude, we have to admit the obvious. We can teach what the correct principles are, but we can't make anybody follow them. (We have a hard enough time making the correct choices ourselves.) Whatever we measure ourselves against, it can't be that. In self-evaluation, as in so much else, we are thrown back upon our own resources—our own private successes, our own much-lamented failures.

But that's the way the plan was supposed to work. The gospel teaches us that we each exist in a strong web of family, the generations supporting each other vertically, the widening rings of our brothers and sisters and their families spreading out horizontally. But within that web, each one of us is an individual with a unique and private relationship with our Father in Heaven. In the end, the only self-evaluation that can be valid is the one formed out of that relationship, because only our Heavenly Father can see how far we are coming along the long road to perfection, and only he can understand and forgive the inevitable detours we all take along the way.

Oddly enough, that's one of the hardest things to have faith in. Repentance as a principle is the kind of thing you diagram on the blackboard in a Primary class. But believing that though you may have done something that was wrong, deeply and shamefully wrong, through the power of repentance it can be wholly erased, just like the words on that blackboard—really believing that is surprisingly difficult. It's even hard to trust that all the petty stuff—the half-truths that shade off into something worse, the spontaneous selfishness, the obligations not fully met and then glossed over—can be wiped away. Instead, we waste today's precious time in playing old tapes over and over in our heads, wishing we could somehow run events backward and make right whatever it was we messed up on. In purely mortal terms, we face the implacable truth that time past is time past and that all the wishing in the world won't unreel it.

With the light of the gospel, the situation is entirely different. The tool of repentance is there all the time, within our reach. It won't make what happened disappear, but it will lift the burden of our guilt and hopelessness from our shoulders.

We can start over, wiser because of what we have learned but not continually burdened by it.

After all, that's exactly what Christ's sacrifice was all about—to give us precisely that incomparable gift. Repentance is not necessarily an easy process—there's a lot more to repentance than muttering, "I'm sorry. That wasn't right, was it?"—but once accomplished, in some way that we don't wholly understand, whatever it is that we have done can be set aside. Virtually any mistake, however drastic, can be repented of, and once the cleansing of repentance is accomplished, it's over. Really, truly over.

That's the part that's hard to believe, and perversely, often the hardest part is letting go of the guilt. You've done something wrong; you know it was wrong. There may have been all kinds of ramifications for yourself and others, and maybe the others knew that it all stemmed from whatever it was you did, but maybe they didn't know. Maybe you were able to go back and straighten out some of the consequences in the process of repenting, but it's quite probable, life moving on as it does, that some things cannot now be fixed. So how can it all be made right and be forgiven? It doesn't seem fair that it can.

It's a question not only of how the Lord can forgive you but of how you can forgive yourself. And yet anyone can see that permanently berating yourself for past errors is obviously unproductive. Once again, it is only faith that can make the difference—faith that when we are promised forgiveness, that's exactly what we get, and the fact that our hearts are lightened and we can move past whatever it was without a backward glance is not a sign that we are shallow and irresponsible. It's precisely so that we can have that freedom that Christ took the permanent consequences of our sins and paid for them with his own life.

Jesus recognized that we might have a problem understanding forgiveness. One of his most frequently retold parables, the story of the prodigal son, deals with all those issues—forgiveness and fairness and redemption—and there have been volumes of commentary written about this parable, because the whole mechanism of forgiveness is so elusively mysterious. What about the elder brother? (Some of us are particularly keenly interested in him, because those of us who are living relatively orderly lives feel we might quite reasonably identify with him.) It would seem more appropriate to all of us would-be elder brothers if the prodigal son were not welcomed home quite so wholeheartedly—and yet the irony is that all of us are the prodigal in one way or another and are wholly dependent on exactly that welcome to find our own way home.

Whether our individual primary sin is self-righteousness or something flashier, we need to have that potential for a fresh start. Maybe we never will understand, from our perspective here, how forgiveness works, but there's an eternal perspective we can't see. What we do know is that for here and now what has been repented of is over, and we can let loose of the guilt and find something more useful to do with that energy. Goodness knows, there is plenty of the Lord's work that could use some extra energy right here and now, and we can reserve the whole question of fairness, elder brother and all, until that unlikely day when we have the leisure, and the perspective, to sort it all through.

In the final analysis, after all, it isn't what we think of ourselves that counts. We have to turn in faith and trust to our Heavenly Father, who knows what we're good at, and what trips us up from time to time, and where our most serious obstacles lie. Like stubborn two-year-olds or rebellious adolescents, we sometimes try to grab the reins into our own hands, not recognizing that only by turning ourselves over to conscious acquiescence with the Lord's pattern for our lives will we be able to find the peace we're grasping for.

What we're trying to measure, really, boils down to a matter of how close we are coming to the perfection that will enable us to once again feel wholly at home in his presence. Some days it feels as if we are very far off indeed; some days (and they're the happy, contented days when doing the right things seems natural and easy) we can almost see around the bend in the road that will lead us back to where we belong.

It's a long road, and some of us inevitably are traveling down it faster than others. Some of us take more detours; some of us get tired and sit down for a while. Perhaps what we need to verify is not so much how fast we're getting there as that we're heading steadfastly in the right direction, and that we keep a hand available to help our companions on the way. Sometimes our companions are the people we love best, our families and our dearest friends; sometimes our companions are strangers we may never see again. Sometimes what's needed is a mother's shoulder, and sometimes it's the old familiar casserole delivered to the door, and sometimes we're not quite sure what is needed, and we have to rely on the ready resource of prayer to find out. Sometimes we bump up against the stranger and then move off in separate directions, never realizing that we were each tools in the Lord's hands to bless one another.

Maybe being able to work out exactly where on that road we are would be comforting, but maybe one of the conditions of this world is uncertainty, and maybe the only sure guide is the peace in our hearts when we are in harmony with what the Lord would have us do. "Peace I leave with you, my peace I give unto you," Christ promised us (John 14:27). Maybe that unmistakable sense of peacefulness is the only instrument flexible enough to guide us in all the amazing variations of our individual lives.

A report card might be nice, but we have grown up enough to know that everything in life is not reducible to the simplicity of a grade. Perhaps it's just as well.

8

On Perfection

I have to admit that on the average wet Wednesday I'm not usually thinking a lot about perfection, really—it's more the imperfections that have my attention, my own as well as those of the people I live with and am extremely fond of on happier days.

On wet Wednesdays I seem to slap around the house, getting progressively more irritated every time I encounter something else that somebody has dropped somewhere before wandering off. There are shoes and odd socks (what do they *do* with the other sock? I don't seem to remember people walking around with one on and one off); there are mail-order catalogs that my adolescent daughters have been inspecting all over the house, and newspapers, and envelopes ripped open—the contents apparently having been taken elsewhere. There are toys and parts of toys. Why don't they ever pick up after themselves, and why can't I seem to teach them to pick things up? On wet Wednesdays it all feels very futile.

On wet Wednesdays, when the phone rings it doesn't ever seem to be somebody I want to talk to. Well, I suppose if I'm honest I have to admit that it probably sometimes is, but that's not what I notice. What I notice are the phone calls reminding me of upcoming obligations or inquiring about something I've forgotten to do—or the dentist confirming the appointment for the next day. On wet Wednesdays I discover the stained shirt that went through the dryer (why can't I learn to check the laundry thoroughly when I'm sorting it?) and the overdue bill that somehow didn't get put in the appropriate cubbyhole on the desk. On wet Wednesdays the disposal makes ominous grinding noises (what got dropped down there this time?) and stops dead.

It's on that sort of day that I am inclined to fantasize gloomily about the woman I should be—the woman I would be if I just followed all the well-meant advice and did everything I am counseled to do in all the lessons and generally stayed on top of things. I can picture her clearly.

She wouldn't get cross, she wouldn't get discouraged, and she would never waste time. With no fuss, she would meet all the expectations. Were she to step into my shoes (which would have to be polished, naturally), the bits and pieces of my life would immediately fall into order, tidily organized and obedient.

My jeans might need a wash, but she would be forever immaculate. All the beds would be made first thing in the morning, and her ironing basket would be empty. The garden would be well kept, whatever the season. Her cooking would be economical and nutritious, and she would have the flair of presenting it so that the family ate happily, instead of poking things around on their plates with their forks and asking suspicious questions. She wouldn't have any half-finished projects pushed way to the back of a drawer. She would never have to throw together a Sunday School or Primary lesson in the last couple of hours before giving it, and she would always have her visiting teaching done by the middle of the month. She wouldn't have to be asked to give compassionate service; she would already be aware of who needed help and whether what was needed might be the covered dish or a couple of hours of baby-sitting. No matter how busy the day, she would always find time and serenity to read the scriptures thoughtfully, and when she prayed, her mind would never wander.

She would always have a genuine smile. The unavoidable repetition of ordinary living—laundry, meal preparation, cleaning up the place—would never get to her. She would capably manage whatever job fell to her lot and arrange her time so that work demands never infringed on family responsibilities or vice versa. Her children would never seem irritating to her, and she would always understand her husband. She would never yell.

Her whole house would be clean and orderly and stay that way. She would never have to make half-serious pacts with a friend that if she were struck by lightning, the friend would get to the house and deal with the worst of the clutter before the Relief Society arrived. If unexpected disaster did befall, there would not be a loose end left for the good sisters to take care of—not a thing for them to do but to put their casseroles down on the shining kitchen counter and sigh in admiring tribute.

Now, it's not as if I don't know how to go about cultivating any of the virtues on that whole list, except maybe the part about getting the family to eat everything placed in front of them. I even *do* do the rest of those things, here and there, from time to time. If perfection for me, living the life I live, consisted of matching up to the example of my fantasy, I could honestly say that I have flashes of it. But how do we get from the flashes to the shining promise of the goal?

My first impulse, particularly on the discouraging days, is to kick the furniture sulkily and declare that perfection is too hard a goal. Nobody can live up to that, not all the time. (And Satan, keeping me company, whispers encouragement. "Of course it's too hard. You can't expect people to be their best all the time. People get fed up sometimes. They can't be expected to just keep trying. It's unnatural.") What about getting tired? What about getting along with other people, who might not be as righteous as they should be? What about thinking about yourself sometimes? Wouldn't being perfect mean doing all the work? It just all sounds so *hard*, so dreadfully difficult to maintain.

But would it be? I wonder how much my point of view is skewed by my present imperfections. Peter's imperfections distorted his point of view, of course, when he sank into the water that up until then had been supporting him as he walked in faith toward Jesus. At first, he had such perfect trust that he stepped out of the boat onto the water when his Lord told him to come, and he walked unafraid across the surface, just as Jesus himself was walking on the water toward their boat. But then Peter started to worry about the howling wind and the strangeness of what he was doing, and, losing his trust, he began to sink. (See Matthew 14:22–31.) Maybe if we had the same unquestioning faith and trust that Peter started out with, we could walk in perfection.

Maybe we don't realize how much more complicated and difficult we make our own ordinary, imperfect lives when we stubbornly make wrong choices. After all, most of the commandments rise out of common sense. Life is inherently more pleasurable if we love one another freely, without preconditions. Dishonesty, violence, and immorality make a mess out of the lives not only of the perpetrators but also of everybody who gets involved with these people. The Word of Wisdom works: it may not cure everything that might be wrong with you, but steadfast adherence certainly will bring you both physical and spiritual blessings. Paying your tithes and offerings faithfully is one way of developing financial responsibility, and as Jesus observed centuries ago, "Where your treasure is, there will your heart be also" (Matthew 6:21). People whose treasure is invested in the work of the Lord are generally less tense and anxious than people who place their faith in vaults.

Maybe if we could just trustfully turn to the Lord, as Peter did, and go ahead and do what we've been told—ignoring all our reasons why it won't work—we'd find that things would fall into place and that the difficulties would tend to melt harmlessly away.

After all, we wouldn't be alone, any more than Peter was alone out there on the water. Christ was with him then, and he is with us now. Our job has never been to achieve perfection on our own. Oh, Satan tries to make us believe that that's what we have to do. When we are faltering along the tightrope suspended high over the safety net, Satan tells us, "There you are, all by yourself, and then they expect you to do everything right."

Of all his lies, that is the greatest. Never for a moment are we alone, unless by our own free agency we choose to be. Christ has promised us his strength, his comfort, and his love, and only by a deliberate decision to turn away can we lose those promises. As long as we trust in him and as long as we are trying to do his will, he will be there. He has promised us over and over that our failures cannot estrange us from him, as long as we are willing to try again and as long as we trust in him.

Trust in the Lord comes first, but we also need the faith to trust in the strengths the Lord has given us. Having told us that perfection should be our goal, the Lord will provide a process—if we work at it—for perfection to come about. Each of us has been given precisely the strengths we individually will need to return home as perfected creatures. We've each been given a different combination, and each of us must find our way back by our own unique path. Sooner or later we each have to discover that we can learn from each other but that copying others—like an unprepared student cheating on an exam—simply isn't possible. We each have to reach down within ourselves to find our own possibilities, and all the doubt and discouragement that comes along with the reaching process is part of what we have to learn to manage. Working for perfection is grown-up business; we can't expect to get very far if we sit down and glower or drum our heels with childish impatience when things go wrong.

It's not an overnight business, either. We are surrounded with distractions and temptations; keeping our minds on what we're trying to do is the hardest part of all. We have to face the humbling fact that we're not good enough now, and the reality that recognizing we're not good enough is not the happiest way to feel. It isn't meant to be. If not being good enough were a perfectly satisfactory condition, what on earth would motivate us to stretch to become anything more? Maybe that's why we take our biggest steps when we face our greatest problems: our discontent drives us forward. I wonder if it hurts the caterpillar to turn into the chrysalis, or the chrysalis to burst open to free the butterfly? Whether it does or not, the creature can't stop developing. To try to cling to either of those stages, so clearly designed to be transitional, would mean death.

We are in a transitional stage, too. Maybe the dissatisfaction and the unhappiness of the discouraging days are the spurs the Lord gives us to urge us to move forward and to keep trying to find the ways to come ever closer to him. Maybe without those spurs it would be too easy to trudge along unchallenged, stirring the soup and folding the socks, doing just enough to get by and not bothering to look around much at anybody else's needs or anything going on outside the boundaries of our own confortable ruts. We would return to our Father like amiable cattle, not having gone far and not having learned much, either.

Could it be that the emptiness we sometimes feel on those wet Wednesdays, as we stare aimlessly out of the kitchen window or across an impersonal office, is meant to be a reminder that we are creatures designed for eternity and that we are away from home only on a temporary assignment? It might happen that some of the duties we are given—and expected to learn to do better—seem as pointless right now as elementary piano exercises often seem when you start taking lessons. But should you finally master the skills of playing the piano properly, it is in large part because your fingers and your mind have learned coordination through those same repetitive piano exercises. Could it be that duties as ordinary and unexciting as getting the laundry done on schedule and teaching reverence to our children on a wriggly Sunday will turn out to be the cornerstones of skills we can't even imagine now?

If that's all true, maybe there's more point to the wet Wednesdays than I can see now, harnessed to mortality and my short perspective. Maybe when I try to imagine what perfection would really be like in my life (my life, which is presently only perfect in being perfectly ordinary) the closest I get is imagining that wet Wednesday fantasy of mine, that aggravating imaginary woman who would do everything right. Predictably, what I think catches my attention most is not that she is so effortlessly competent at the ordinary skills that give me trouble, but that she remains serenely on the path of virtue when I so easily lapse into expediency and self-indulgence.

Mostly I think about her as a reproachful presence, reminding me of all the ways in which I fail. She sees the needs of others first; I get too absorbed with my own. She meets her obligations with gladness; I grumble and postpone getting down to mine. She prays as naturally as she breathes; I have to keep recapturing my attention, like a wandering toddler. Her perfection dances in my mind, an uncomfortable contrast to my own ungainly imperfections. But should it necessarily be that way? Is there another way of using that fantasy, perhaps?

We don't have very many heroes, or heroines, in our time. I guess the problem is that we would love to have some, but they make us suspicious. No sooner is a candidate thrown up before us than we scurry around, checking every angle for flaws. It's as if we are convinced that no one can truly be larger than life-size, and so we search for evidence that we are right. We want to believe in the possibility of being better and finer, and yet, jealously, we are reluctant to believe that anyone else can be this way, when we ourselves find it so difficult.

Maybe the fantasy could be one way of resolving that dilemma. I know she's not real, but even so, she can be a reminder of my possibilities. Thinking about her reminds me that there is the potential for perfection in the absolutely ordinary details that make up my daily life. Perfection needn't be a remote, celestial hypothesis: it could exist in the most unethereal, mundane details of my responsibilities—dealing with my children with tenderness and charity, truly making myself a resource available to those people whose lives touch mine, holding down a job with absolute honesty and fidelity, maintaining a marriage and fulfilling not only the letter but also the spirit of the vows we took, and doing my share in carrying out the daily business of the Lord's work on this earth.

The heroines, or would-be heroines, that the world serves up have little to do with me. The beauties of the stage and screen, Princess Diana, and Mother Teresa are individually and collectively totally unrelated to the kind of life given to me to lead. Maybe I should take my fantasy as my "heroine," an expression of what I may grow to be. I can't see myself succeeding at it by tomorrow lunchtime or even next week sometime, but there's no hurry. This job is one for a lifetime. Perhaps a first step is to stop looking at my fantasy as a reproach, and see her as a pattern.

Maybe it would work even on the wet Wednesdays. After all, I know I have flashes of succeeding the way she does: maybe I could stop staring moodily out of the window and try stretching out some of those flashes. Maybe instead of feeling badgered because I have a list of calls to make but haven't got around to making them, I could do what she would do and get out the list and get started. Maybe there's somebody on that list who needs to hear from me, and maybe there's some service I could render—I'm certainly not accomplishing much by glooming around at home.

Wouldn't it be odd if the secret was as simple as that—that what we need to do most on the discouraging days, the wet Wednesdays, is to simply stop brooding about things as they are and start taking practical steps to make them change? Would it help to remember that each of us is a daughter of God, with her own strengths and her own challenges, and that we're not in a race with anyone else?

Could we try focusing on where we're going and worry less about where we are, and along the way, remember to enjoy the experiences we hope to take with us? After all, we've been promised joy—the everlasting happiness that lights up our lives and gives us a glimpse of the life that is waiting for us. We know, each of us, that every day is not a wet Wednesday and that we experience that joy at times, even now. Remember the happy times, the times when the whole family is caught up in perfect harmony? Remember the comfortable reassurance of glancing across the room at your husband and knowing exactly what he's thinking from his smile? Remember the heartwarming conversations when you and a friend are so much in harmony that you can practically finish each other's sentences?

And the best is yet to come. Someday we will have the chance to be welcomed back into our Father's presence. We won't be the same spirits he sent out: all the good times and the troubles and the confusion and the love we have known on this earth will have changed us as certainly as our own children change from the babies we hold against our shoulders to the adults who come home to visit bringing babies of their own. If we've fulfilled our assignments as we were meant to do, we will be wiser and more trusting; having tasted the bitterness of disobedience, we will have learned a deeper appreciation of righteousness. Maybe then perfection will seem like the automatic next step, as easy and comfortable as an old friend's smile.

Maybe then the wet Wednesdays will be a vague memory, and, looking back, we'll wonder why they ever seemed so daunting. After all, the discouragement and the loneliness were only temporary. The Lord's love was always around us, ready to help us hold on until the clouds moved past. When we look back and remember, as we're moving forward into whatever comes next, we'll realize that he was always there for us.

We can even begin to know it now. So what if today began as a wet Wednesday? Wrapping myself in that eternal love, I can pick up the dishcloth—or the file on my desk—and get back to the ordinary, daily business of meeting my responsibilities, with the sure knowledge that, by meeting them, I can grow into the felicity of really being good enough. And along the way there will be the flashes of true joy to sustain me, and all of us— maybe a spontaneous hug from a child, or the satisfaction of learning something new, or maybe a moment of shared delight with a friend. "I am come that they might have life," Jesus promised us, "and that they might have it more abundantly" (John 10:10).

Even on a wet Wednesday—look! Here comes the sun!